HOUGHTON MIFFLIN HARCOURT

SOCIAL STUDIES

NEW YORK CITY

COMMUNITIES NEAR AND FAR

Program Authors

Dr. Herman J. Viola

Dr. Sarah Witham Bednarz

Dr. Carlos E. Cortés

Dr. Cheryl Jennings

Dr. Mark C. Schug

Dr. Charles S. White

Visit **Education Place®**

www.eduplace.com/kids

 HOUGHTON MIFFLIN HARCOURT

Authors

Senior Author
Dr. Herman J. Viola
Curator Emeritus
Smithsonian Institution

Dr. Cheryl Jennings
Project Director
Florida Institute of Education
University of North Florida

Dr. Sarah Witham Bednarz
Associate Professor, Geography
Texas A&M University

Dr. Mark C. Schug
Professor and Director
Center for Economic Education
University of Wisconsin, Milwaukee

Dr. Carlos E. Cortés
Professor Emeritus, History
University of California, Riverside

Dr. Charles S. White
Associate Professor
School of Education
Boston University

Program Consultants

Philip J. Deloria
Associate Professor
Department of History and
Program in American Studies
University of Michigan

Lucien Ellington
UC Professor of Education and Asia
Program Co-Director
University of Tennessee, Chattanooga

Thelma Wills Foote
Associate Professor
University of California

Stephen J. Fugita
Distinguished Professor
Psychology and Ethnic Studies
Santa Clara University

Charles C. Haynes
Senior Scholar
First Amendment Center

Ted Hemmingway
Professor of History
The Florida Agricultural &
Mechanical University

Douglas Monroy
Professor of History
The Colorado College

Lynette K. Oshima
Assistant Professor
Department of Language, Literacy
and Sociocultural Studies and Social
Studies Program Coordinator
University of New Mexico

Jeffrey Strickland
Assistant Professor, History
University of Texas Pan American

Clifford E. Trafzer
Professor of History and
American Indian Studies
University of California

Printed in the U.S.A.

ISBN: 978-0-547-68917-3

1 2 3 4 5 6 7 8 9 10   0914   20 19 18 17 16 15 14 13 12 11
4500303622   ^ B C D E F G

New York State Social Studies Standards
Elementary School

STANDARD 1

HISTORY OF THE UNITED STATES AND NEW YORK

Students will use a variety of intellectual skills to demonstrate their understanding of major ideas, eras, themes, developments, and turning points in the history of the United States and New York.

1.1 The study of New York State and United States history requires an analysis of the development of American culture, its diversity and multicultural context, and the ways people are unified by many values, practices, and traditions.

1.2 Important ideas, social and cultural values, beliefs, and traditions from New York State and United States history illustrate the connections and interactions of people and events across time and from a variety of perspectives.

1.3 The study about the major social, political, economic, cultural, and religious developments in New York State and United States history involves learning about the important roles and contributions of individuals and groups.

1.4 The skills of historical analysis include the ability to: explain the significance of historical evidence, weigh the importance, reliability, and validity of evidence, understand the concept of multiple causation, and understand the importance of changing and competing interpretations of different historical developments.

STANDARD 2

WORLD HISTORY

Students will use a variety of intellectual skills to demonstrate their understanding of major ideas, eras, themes, developments, and turning points in world history and examine the broad sweep of history from a variety of perspectives.

2.1 The study of world history requires an understanding of world cultures and civilizations, including an analysis of important ideas, social and cultural values, beliefs, and traditions. This study also examines the human condition and the connections and interactions of people across time and space and the ways different people view the same event or issue from a variety of perspectives.

2.2 Establishing timeframes, exploring different periodizations, examining themes across time and within cultures, and focusing on important turning points in world history help organize the study of world cultures and civilizations.

2.3 The study of the major social, political, cultural, and religious developments in world history involves learning about the important roles and contributions of individuals and groups.

2.4 The skills of historical analysis include the ability to investigate differing and competing interpretations of the theories of history, hypothesize about why interpretations change over time, explain the importance of historical evidence, and understand the concepts of change and continuity over time.

STANDARD 3

GEOGRAPHY

Students will use a variety of intellectual skills to demonstrate their understanding of the geography of the interdependent world in which we live — local, national, and global — including the distribution of people, places, and environments over the Earth's surface.

3.1 Geography can be divided into six essential elements, which can be used to analyze important historic, geographic, economic, and environmental questions and issues. These six elements include: the world in spatial terms, places and regions, physical settings (including natural resources), human systems, environment and society, and the use of geography.

3.2 Geography requires the development and application of the skills of asking and answering geography questions, analyzing theories of geography, and acquiring and organizing geographic information.

STANDARD 4

ECONOMICS

Students will use a variety of intellectual skills to demonstrate their understanding of how the United States and other societies develop economic systems and associated institutions to allocate scarce resources, how major decision-making units function in the U.S. and other national economies, and how an economy solves the scarcity problem through market and non-market mechanisms.

4.1 The study of economics requires an understanding of major economic concepts and systems, the principles of economic decision making, and the interdependence of economies and economic systems throughout the world.

4.2 Economics requires the development and application of the skills needed to make informed and well-reasoned economic decisions in daily and national life.

STANDARD 5

CIVICS, CITIZENSHIP, AND GOVERNMENT

Students will use a variety of intellectual skills to demonstrate their understanding of the necessity for establishing governments, the governmental system of the United States and other nations, the United States Constitution, the basic civic values of American constitutional democracy, and the roles, rights, and responsibilities of citizenship, including avenues of participation.

5.1 The study of civics, citizenship, and government involves learning about political systems; the purposes of government and civic life; and the differing assumptions held by people across time and place regarding power, authority, governance, and law.

5.2 The state and federal governments established by the Constitutions of the United States and the State of New York embody basic civic values (such as justice, honesty, self-discipline, due process, equality, majority rule with respect for minority rights, and respect for self, others, and property), principles, and practices and establish a system of shared and limited government.

5.3 Central to civics and citizenship is an understanding of the roles of the citizen within American constitutional democracy and the scope of a citizen's rights and responsibilities.

5.4 The study of civics and citizenship requires the ability to probe ideas and assumptions, ask and answer analytical questions, take a skeptical attitude toward questionable arguments, evaluate evidence, formulate rational conclusions, and develop and refine participatory skills.

Our Community's Geography

1

New York City Over Time

54

Urban, Suburban, and Rural Communities 106

Rights, Rules, and Responsibilities

150

Our Rules

1. Take turns.
2. Work quietly.
3. Be kind to others.

Resources

Features

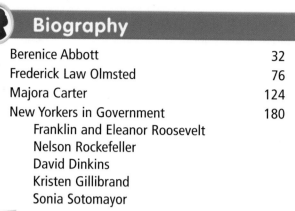

Biography

Infographics

Primary Sources

Skill Lessons

Take a step-by-step approach to learning and practicing key social studies skills.

Visual Learning

Constitution Day

Our country is a special place. One reason is because of the freedoms people have here. Citizens of the United States are free to say and print what they think, as long as the words do not hurt others. People are free to join groups. These freedoms are described in a paper called the United States Constitution.

The Constitution is a written plan that says what the nation's government can and cannot do. It was written more than 200 years ago by a group of leaders. They signed the Constitution on September 17, 1787. Today we celebrate Constitution Day and Citizenship Day during the week of September 17.

Activity

Make a Picture Dictionary The Constitution gives you many freedoms, such as freedom to speak and write, freedom to believe what you want, and freedom to meet with groups. Make a picture dictionary that shows the freedoms you have in the United States.

Unit 1

Our Community's Geography

The Big Idea

How does geography influence where people choose to live and why?

What to Know

✔ How do maps help people find locations?

✔ What communities are near where you live?

✔ What kinds of landforms and bodies of water does the United States have?

✔ What are the land and water like in New York City?

✔ Why are waterways and islands important to New York City?

✔ What natural resources do people use? How do they use them?

New York City has a unique landscape.

NEW JERSEY

Upper New York Bay

Governors Island

Staten Island

NEW YORK

NEW JERSEY

Long Island Sound

Bronx

The East River separates the city's boroughs.

Manhattan

Hudson River

Queens

East River

Brooklyn

Jamaica Bay

Lower New York Bay

North
West — East
South

ATLANTIC OCEAN

Reading Social Studies

Main Idea and Details

Why It Matters When you read for information, look for the main ideas and important details.

Learn the Skill

Good paragraphs have a main idea and details.

■ The main idea is the most important part of what you are reading.

■ The details explain the main idea.

Read the paragraph below.

Main Idea
Detail

New York City is a fun place to visit. There is a lot to see and do. You can visit the city's beautiful parks, interesting museums, and tall buildings. New York City has many bodies of water. You can travel by walking, driving, taking a train, or even riding a boat!

Practice the Skill

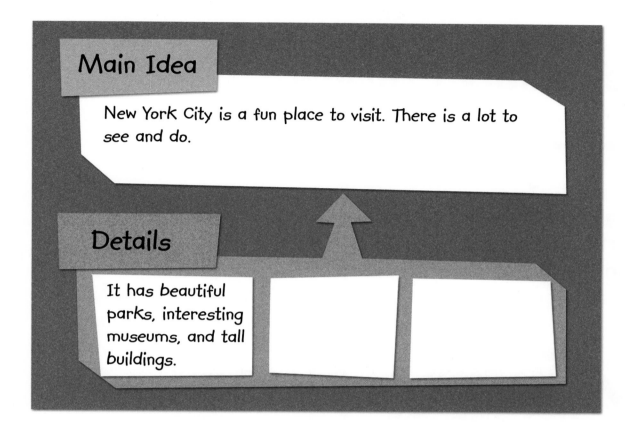

Main Idea

New York City is a fun place to visit. There is a lot to see and do.

Details

It has beautiful parks, interesting museums, and tall buildings.

This chart shows the main idea and one detail from what you just read. Copy the chart and complete it.

Apply the Skill

As you read this unit, look for main ideas and details about how land and water affect people.

Vocabulary Preview

globe

A **globe** is a model of Earth. You can find continents and oceans on a globe. **page 14**

cardinal directions

Cardinal directions are the main directions of north, south, east, and west. **page 16**

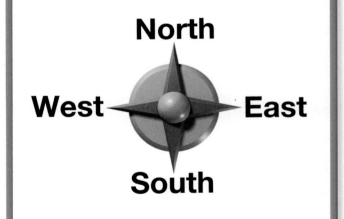

North

West   East

South

landform

A **landform** is one of the shapes of land found on Earth. A mountain is a landform. **page 24**

natural resource

Water is an important natural resource. A **natural resource** is something in nature that people can use. **page 42**

 visit www.eduplace.com/nycssp/

All Kinds of Maps

What to Know
How do maps help people find locations?

Vocabulary
map
location
community
boundary

Reading Skill
Main Idea and Details

Before You Read
Think about where you live. What places are near your home?

Maps Show Locations
A **map** is a flat drawing that shows where places are. You can use maps to find the location of your school or home. A **location** tells where a place is. On the map below, the school's location is near the park. It is also on Central Avenue.

main idea

What is the location of the market?

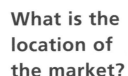

Mapmakers can use photographs taken from above to make maps.

Making Maps

People who make maps use special tools. Long ago, mapmakers drew maps on paper. They used tools such as a compass to find locations of places. Today, mapmakers study photographs taken from the sky to find locations. They use computers to make maps.

(★) main idea

✓ **Reading Check** **Main Idea and Details** What is the purpose of a map?

How We Use Maps

There are many kinds of maps. They show different information. Some maps show small areas, such as a park or a community. A **community** is a place where groups of people live. Other maps show larger areas, such as New York City or New York State.

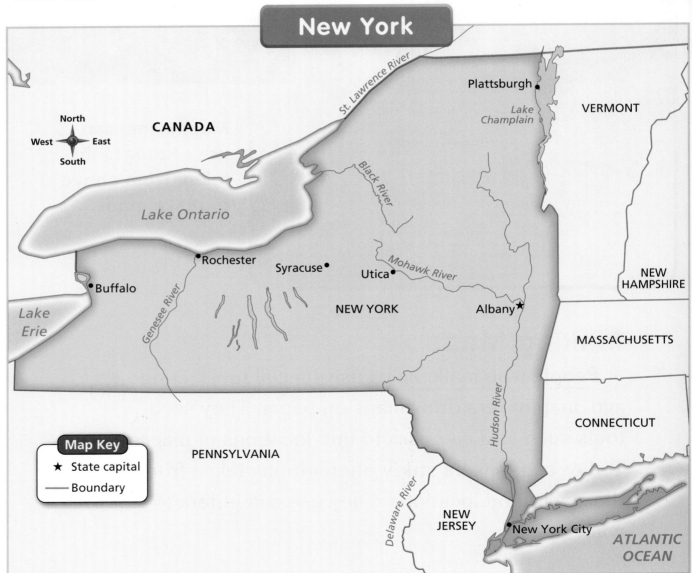

New York

Plattsburgh

VERMONT

Lake Champlain

St. Lawrence River

CANADA

North
West — East
South

Black River

Lake Ontario

NEW HAMPSHIRE

Rochester

Syracuse

Utica

Mohawk River

Albany

Buffalo

Genesee River

NEW YORK

MASSACHUSETTS

Lake Erie

Hudson River

CONNECTICUT

Map Key

★ State capital
— Boundary

PENNSYLVANIA

Delaware River

NEW JERSEY

New York City

ATLANTIC OCEAN

Skill **Reading Maps** What is the location of New York State?

New Jersey

New York

Lines on a map show boundaries. A **boundary** is where a place ends. Your city and your community have boundaries. Sometimes a boundary can run along a body of water. The Hudson River is part of the boundary between New York and New Jersey.

✓ **Reading Check** **Classify** What kind of boundary separates parts of New York and New Jersey?

Lesson Review

❶ **What to Know** How do maps help people find locations?

❷ **Vocabulary** What is the **location** of your school?

❸ **Main Idea and Details** What tools do mapmakers today use to make maps?

❹ **Art Activity** Draw a map of your school. Show how you get from your classroom to the cafeteria.

New York World's Fair 1939

Have you ever been to a theme park or a festival? Did you use a map to find your way around? In 1939, a World's Fair was held in New York City. Visitors to the fair saw what "The World of Tomorrow" might look like.

This map uses picture symbols to show the locations of buildings at the fair. Many symbols look bigger on the map than they are in real life.

This 40-foot tall cash register showed the number of people who came to the fair each day.

These buildings are called the Trylon and the Perisphere. Here, visitors looked at a model of a city of the future. The buildings became symbols for the fair.

Activities

1. **Talk About It** How would visitors to the World's Fair use this map?

2. **Write About It** Describe which places you would have visited if you had gone to the 1939 New York World's Fair.

 Go Digital Visit Education Place for more primary sources. www.eduplace.com/nycssp/

Skillbuilder

Review: Maps and Globes

▶ **Vocabulary**

globe
ocean
continent

A **globe** is a model of Earth. It shows that Earth is round like a ball. A world map is a flat picture of Earth. You can use a globe or a map to find continents, oceans, and other places.

Learn the Skill

Step 1 Look at the globe. Much of the world is covered by large areas of water called **oceans**. They are usually colored blue on globes and maps.

Step 2 Find the Atlantic Ocean on the globe and on the map. In what way is the ocean the same on the globe and the map?

Step 3 **Continents** are the big areas of land you see on a globe or map. Find North America on the globe and the map. Globes and maps show countries, too. Find Canada on the globe and the map.

North Pole

South Pole

Look at the globe and the map. Then follow the directions.

1 Compare the globe and the map. Tell how they are alike and different.

2 Look at the globe and find the continent and country where you live. Then find them on the map. Write their names in your notebook.

World Map

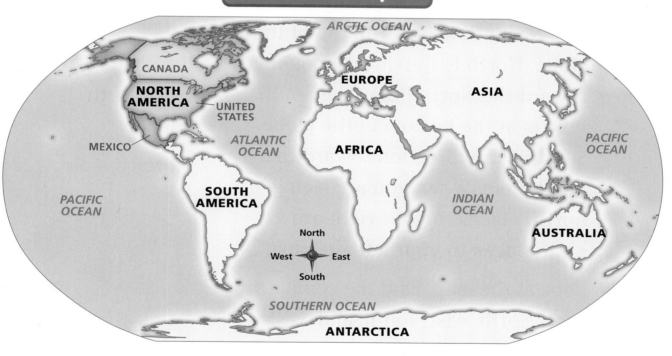

Name the seven continents and the five oceans you see on the map.

Skillbuilder

Review: Symbols and Directions

Directions help people find places on globes and maps. A **compass rose** shows directions.

Symbols are pictures that stand for real things. Most maps use symbols. A map key explains what the symbols stand for.

Learn the Skill

Step 1 The North Pole is at the top of the globe. North is the direction going toward the North Pole. The South Pole is at the bottom of the globe. South is the direction toward the South Pole. When you are facing north, places to your right are east. Places to your left are west.

Step 2 Look at the map. Find the compass rose. North, east, south, and west are the **cardinal directions**.

Step 3 Look at the map key. The symbol for forest is a tree. Find the symbol for forest on the map.

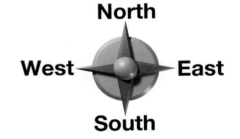

North
West   East
South

North Pole

South Pole

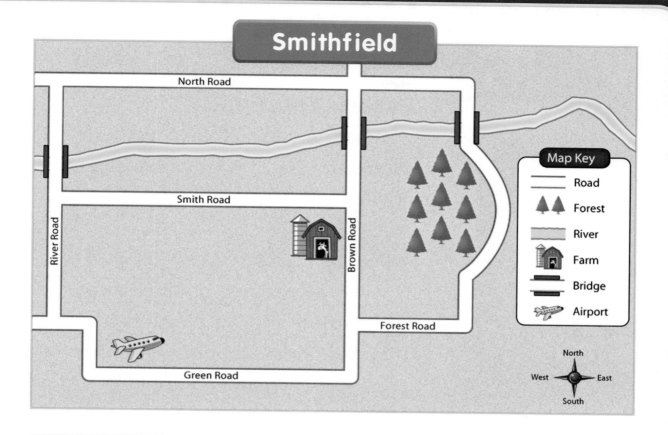

Smithfield

North Road

Smith Road

River Road

Brown Road

Forest Road

Green Road

Map Key
Road
Forest
River
Farm
Bridge
Airport

North
West — East
South

Practice the Skill

Look at the map. Then follow the directions.

1 Look at the map key. Describe the symbol for road.

2 Look at the river symbol on the map key. Find the river on the map. What is a symbol that touches the river?

3 Use the compass rose. What is east of the farm?

Apply the Skill

Make a map of your classroom. Use a compass rose to show directions.

Lesson 2

Where You Live

▶ **What to Know**

What communities are near where you live?

▶ **Vocabulary**

citizen
borough
country
state

◎ **Reading Skill**

Classify

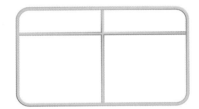

Before You Read

What do you call the neighborhood where you live? Do you know the rest of your address?

Neighborhood and City

A city is made up of different parts. One of these parts is a neighborhood. Tara and her neighbors are citizens of a neighborhood called Jackson Heights. A **citizen** is a person who belongs to a place. Jackson Heights is located near other neighborhoods, such as Astoria, Woodside, and Elmhurst.

main idea ★

Queens, New York City

Astoria

Jackson Heights

Woodside

Elmhurst

Murray Hill

Flushing

Glen Oaks

Maspeth

Ridgewood

Utopia

Jamaica

Cambria Heights

Ozone Park

Rosedale

These and other neighborhoods together make up the borough of Queens. A **borough** is a part of a city. New York City has five boroughs. They are Manhattan, Brooklyn, Queens, the Bronx, and Staten Island. Each borough has its own neighborhoods.

✓**Reading Check** Classify What are some neighborhoods in the borough where you live?

New York City is in the state of New York.

State and Country

Tara is not just a citizen of Jackson Heights, Queens, and New York City. She is also a citizen of New York State and the country of the United States of America. A **country** is a land where people have the same laws and leaders. A **state** is part of a country. The United States is a country made up of 50 states.

main (★) *idea*

Continent

The United States is on the continent of North America. The United States shares North America with two other large countries. They are Canada and Mexico. North America includes many other countries, too.

main idea ★

✔ Reading Check Compare and Contrast What is one way that Mexico and the United States are alike?

North America

ARCTIC OCEAN

CANADA

UNITED STATES

PACIFIC OCEAN

MEXICO

ATLANTIC OCEAN

North
West • East
South

Skill Reading Maps Which oceans touch North America?

Lesson Review

❶ **What to Know** What communities are near where you live?

❷ **Vocabulary** Write a sentence that tells where you live. Use the words **country** and **state** in the sentence.

❸ **Classify** What are the five boroughs of New York City?

❹ **Art Activity** Draw a picture of what your neighborhood looks like.

Skillbuilder

Parts of a Globe

To show locations on a globe, we use the poles, the **equator**, and the **hemispheres**.

▶ **Vocabulary**

equator
hemisphere

Learn the Skill

The North and South poles are imaginary. You cannot see them on Earth. You can only see them on a globe.

North Pole

South Pole

Step 1 The equator is an imaginary line around the middle of Earth. It is halfway between the North Pole and the South Pole.

Step 2 The equator divides Earth into the Northern Hemisphere and the Southern Hemisphere. The Northern Hemisphere is above the equator. The Southern Hemisphere is below the equator.

Step 3 The maps on page 23 show that Earth can also be divided into the Western Hemisphere and the Eastern Hemisphere.

Practice the Skill

Look at the maps. Then follow the directions.

1 Find the continent where you live. Tell which hemispheres you live in.

2 Through which oceans does the equator run?

3 Name two continents in the Eastern Hemisphere.

Western Hemisphere

North Pole

ARCTIC OCEAN

NORTH AMERICA

ATLANTIC OCEAN

Equator

PACIFIC OCEAN

SOUTH AMERICA

SOUTHERN OCEAN

ANTARCTICA

South Pole

Eastern Hemisphere

North Pole

ARCTIC OCEAN

EUROPE

ASIA

AFRICA

PACIFIC OCEAN

Equator

INDIAN OCEAN

AUSTRALIA

SOUTHERN OCEAN

ANTARCTICA

South Pole

Apply the Skill

Draw a globe. Label the equator and the poles.

Land and Water

▶ **What to Know**

What kinds of landforms and bodies of water does the United States have?

▶ **Vocabulary**

landform
valley
island
lake
bay

◎ **Reading Skill**

Compare and Contrast

Before You Read

Think about your community. Is it flat? Is it hilly? Is there a body of water nearby?

Landforms

The land of the United States is shaped in different ways. A **landform** is a kind of land with a special shape. A mountain is a kind of landform. A group of mountains is called a mountain range. Mountain ranges stretch across North America and the United States.

main idea ★

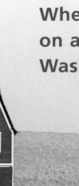

Wheat growing on a plain in Washington State

plain

mountain

valley

Yosemite Valley in California has high mountains on both sides.

A **valley** is low land between mountains. Many valleys in the United States were carved out by rivers running through them long ago. More people farm in valleys than on steep sides of mountains.

A plain is land that is mostly flat. Most of the middle of the United States is covered by plains.

✓ **Reading Check** **Compare and Contrast** How are mountains different from valleys?

Water

Water in the United States comes in many shapes, too. Sometimes land and water together make a landform. An **island** is a landform with water all around it. Other times, land helps shape a body of water. A **lake** is a body of water with land all around it. A **bay** is a body of water that is partly surrounded by land.

(★) main idea

bay

Cape Cod Bay

island

An island in Florida

river

The Colorado River is one of the longest rivers in the United States.

A river is a long, moving body of fresh water. Rivers flow downhill into oceans, lakes, or other rivers.

✓ **Reading Check** **Main Idea and Details** What body of water has land around part of it?

Lesson Review

❶ **What to Know** What kinds of landforms and bodies of water does the United States have?

❷ **Vocabulary** What **landform** is located in the middle of the United States?

❸ **Compare and Contrast** How are lakes different from rivers?

❹ **Writing Activity** Write one or two sentences that tell what you know about land and water in your community.

Landscape of New York City

What to Know
What are the land and water like in New York City?

Vocabulary
hill
canal
harbor

Reading Skill
Main Idea and Details

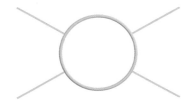

Before You Read
What makes your community a good place to live?

New York City's Features

Each area of New York City is different. Features like land or buildings make places special. Some features are made by nature. They include rivers and hills. A **hill** is land that rises above the land around it. Other features are made by people. They include buildings, statues, roads, and canals. A **canal** is a river made by people.

main idea

New York City has features made by nature and by people.

Canals were made to help move things through the city.

Hills are natural features of the land.

main idea

The land and water of New York City make it a good place for people to live. Long ago, people hunted on and farmed the land. They also fished the rivers and harbor. A **harbor** is an area of deep water that is safe from wind and waves. Even today, people in New York City use the land and water for work and play.

✓ Reading Check Main Idea and Details What are two kinds of features found in New York City?

Plants and Animals

Different plants can be found in New York  City. They include flowers, bushes, grasses, and trees. They grow in parks and along streets. The city's waterways have special plants that grow in and around them.

New York City has animals, too. Most of the animals are small. Common birds include pigeons, sparrows, robins, and cardinals. Bigger birds, such as hawks and owls, build nests in trees or on buildings. Other animals include rabbits, squirrels, and frogs.

Red-tailed hawk

Chipmunk

People can visit the New York Botanical Garden in the Bronx to learn about different plants.

Reading Check **Classify** What is one kind of plant that grows in New York City?

Lesson Review

❶ **What to Know** What are the land and water like in New York City?

❷ **Vocabulary** What is a **harbor**?

❸ **Main Idea and Details** What are some animals found in New York City?

❹ **Art Activity** Draw a picture of a natural feature in your neighborhood. Then draw something made by people.

Berenice Abbott

Berenice Abbott took photographs of New York City in the 1930s. Her pictures show what life was once like in the city.

As a young woman, Abbott went to Paris, France, to learn about taking photographs. When she returned, she was amazed by how much New York City had changed. Many tall buildings were built while she was away.

From 1929 to 1939, Abbott took pictures of the city's new, modern skyline. She liked to show new, tall buildings next to New York City's older buildings. Abbott also showed daily life in New York City. She took pictures of crowded city streets and busy train and bus stations. She showed New Yorkers in their apartments and at work.

Today, Berenice Abbott's photos are some of the only pictures left of New York City buildings that have been torn down.

Activities

1. **Talk About It** Why did Berenice Abbott want to take pictures of New York City?

2. **Draw It** Draw pictures of buildings you would like to photograph.

Waterways and Islands

What to Know

Why are waterways and islands important to New York City?

Vocabulary

geography
waterway
tunnel
transportation

Reading Skill

Compare and Contrast

Before You Read

What bodies of water are near your borough? Do you live on an island?

Waterways Are Important

New York City's geography affects life in the city. **Geography** is what the land and water of a place are like. Waterways are an important part of New York City's geography. A **waterway** is a body of water that boats can use. The city's waterways include rivers, bays, canals, and the ocean.

People can use waterways for having fun.

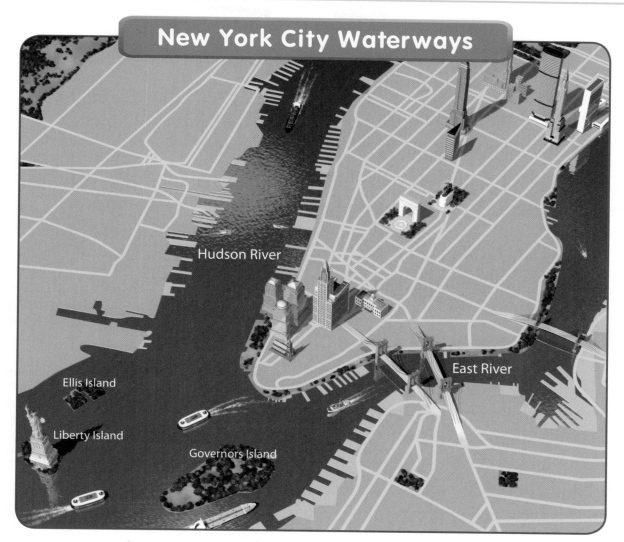

New York City Waterways

Hudson River

East River

Ellis Island

Liberty Island

Governors Island

People in New York City use waterways to travel from place to place. They also use them to move things.

New York City communities are close to waterways. Most communities are on large islands. The Bronx is the only borough not part of a large island. People live in all of these places. There are also several small islands in the city's waterways. People live on some small islands but not on others.

main idea ⭐

Reading Check **Compare and Contrast** How is the Bronx different from the other boroughs?

Connecting Communities

New York City's waterways flow between the islands of the city. <u>Bridges and tunnels connect many of the islands of New York City to each other.</u> A **tunnel** is a path that runs through or under something.

main idea

The George Washington Bridge connects Manhattan to New Jersey.

Different subway lines travel through tunnels and over bridges to all the boroughs of the city.

To travel between communities, people use different kinds of transportation. **Transportation** is the moving of people and things from place to place. Some people cross bridges in cars to go to work or school. Others travel on subways through tunnels or take ferries across the water.

✓ **Reading Check** **Main Idea and Details** What connects the islands of New York City?

Buildings in Brooklyn are not as tall as some in Manhattan, but homes are still built close together.

Geography Affects Communities

Geography affects the size and location of homes and buildings. Manhattan is the smallest borough, but many people live and work there. Because there is little space, buildings are tall and close together. Staten Island has the fewest people. There, homes are built farther apart.

main idea

In Manhattan, people live in tall buildings.

People who live close to the ocean can relax at the beach.

Geography also affects people's jobs and how they have fun. Some people in New York City have jobs on the water. They work on ferries or big tankers. Much of Brooklyn's shore is on the ocean. Many people work at its beaches and harbors.

main idea

✓ Reading Check **Compare and Contrast** What is one way homes in Manhattan are different from those in Staten Island?

Lesson Review

❶ **What to Know** Why are waterways and islands important to New York City?

❷ **Vocabulary** What kinds of **transportation** do you use?

❸ **Compare and Contrast** How are the bridges and tunnels of New York City alike?

❹ **Writing Activity** Write about how geography affects life in your borough.

New York City Bridges and Tunnels

The East River runs between Manhattan and Brooklyn. Engineers have built bridges and tunnels to connect the two boroughs.

The Brooklyn Bridge opened in 1883. It took 13 years to build. It was the first bridge between Manhattan and Brooklyn. Over time, it has been used by people, horse-drawn carriages, trams, cars, and buses.

The Brooklyn-Battery Tunnel was opened in 1950. It crosses under the East River between southern Brooklyn and Manhattan. Even today, it is the longest underwater tunnel for cars in North America.

Brooklyn-Battery Tunnel

More than 1 million people walk or bike across the Brooklyn Bridge every year.

Activities

1. **Talk About It** Why do you think engineers decided to build bridges and tunnels to connect the boroughs?

2. **Draw It** Draw a picture that shows how people might have crossed from Manhattan to Brooklyn before 1883.

Lesson 6 — Using Resources

What to Know

What natural resources do people use? How do they use them?

Vocabulary

natural resource
human resource
environment

Reading Skill

Classify

Before You Read

What do plants need to grow? Most plants need air, soil, water, and sunlight. These things are found in nature.

Kinds of Resources

People use different kinds of resources. Like plants, people use natural resources to live. A **natural resource** is something in nature that people can use. Air, soil, and water are natural resources. So are trees, rubber, coal, and oil.

People use soil to grow fruit and nut trees. Wood from trees is used to build furniture and homes.

Workers are **human resources**.
Human resources can include
nurses, park rangers, police
officers, and bus drivers.

Communities use human and
natural resources in different
ways. Some communities have
farmers who grow food on the
land. Others have carpenters who
build homes using resources such
as wood or stones. Still others
have storeowners who sell things
in stores.

main (★) *idea*

People use water for
drinking, cooking,
washing, and cleaning.

✓ **Reading Check** **Classify** What kind
of resource is a police officer?

Some natural resources can be replaced. If you cut down a tree, you can plant another one.

Changing the Environment

The **environment** is all of the things that people find around them. It includes things in nature, such as land and trees. It also includes things that people add to the land, such as homes and roads.

Tree seedling

People change their environment to meet their needs and make life easier. They cut down trees to make room for homes and roads. They dig tunnels for subways and cars and holes for swimming pools. They take away hills to make the land flat for airports.

main idea

✓ Reading Check **Draw Conclusions** In what way does digging a pool change the environment?

Frame a house

Cut the trees

Clear the land

New York City Resources

People in New York City use both natural and human resources every day. New Yorkers buy food at stores. The soil in which food grows is a natural resource. Workers who move and sell the food are human resources.

main idea ⭐

Workers unload fruit from a truck.

In New York City, food such as fruit comes from all over the world. Farmers in different places grow and gather the fruit. Workers load the fruit on trucks, trains, or ships. The fruit arrives in New York City where it is stored in a building. There, workers load the fruit onto smaller trucks. The trucks carry the fruit to stores. Then, workers put the fruit on the shelves.

main idea

✓ **Reading Check** **Sequence** What happens after farmers gather the fruit?

Customers buy fruit at a produce market.

Lesson Review

❶ **What to Know** What natural resources do people use? How do they use them?

❷ **Vocabulary** List two **natural resources** that you use every day.

❸ **Classify** Think about your school. Make a list of its human resources.

❹ **Art Activity** Draw pictures that show how fruit travels from the farm to the grocery store.

Fun with Social Studies
Land and Water Tic-Tac-Toe

Choose the name of the landform or body of water in each square from the Word Bank. Find the row with three landforms or three bodies of water. List the names.

| bay | hill | river | lake | mountain |
| ocean | plain | valley | island | |

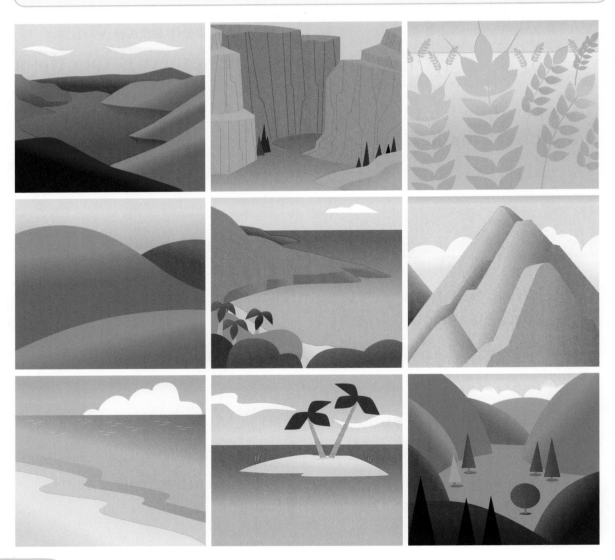

Missing Letters

Each word is missing the same letter. When you find it, use the letter to answer the riddle.

Clue	Word
a drawing that shows where places are	m p
an imaginary line that divides Earth	equ tor
a landform with water all around it	isl nd
a body of water that boats can use	w terw y

What islands are good to eat?

The S ndwich Isl nds

Reading Social Studies

The **main idea** is the most important idea. **Details** are examples or facts that explain the main idea.

 Main Idea and Details

1. Complete the graphic organizer to show that you can identify a main idea and details.

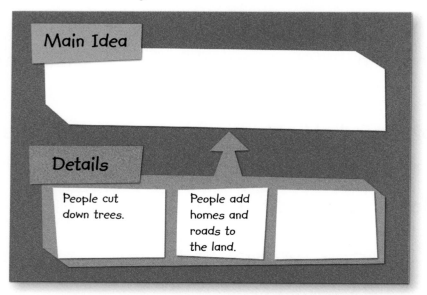

Main Idea

Details

People cut down trees.

People add homes and roads to the land.

 Write About the Big Idea

2. **Write a List** Geography affects where people choose to live and why they choose to live there. Write a list of things that affect where people choose to live.

Vocabulary

Fill in the blanks with the correct words.

In class today, we used a **3.** _____ to find places around the world. Knowing our **4.** _____ helped us find the Hudson River, a **5.** _____ west of New York City. We also found the Catskill Mountains north of New York City. Mountains are one kind of **6.** _____.

A. map (page 8)

B. cardinal directions (page 16)

C. landform (page 24)

D. waterway (page 34)

Facts and Main Ideas

Write a sentence to answer each question.

7. What are the names of New York City's boroughs?

8. What are some New York City features made by people?

9. How do people use waterways?

Critical Thinking

Write a short answer for each question.

10. Analyze Why do you think people make many kinds of maps to show information?

11. Cause and Effect What might happen if people used too much of one natural resource?

12. Find the compass rose. List the cardinal directions.

13. In which direction would you travel from the city to the state park?

14. Which two places are south of the lake?

Parts of a Globe

15. Which two continents are completely in the Southern Hemisphere?

16. Is Europe in the Southern or Northern Hemisphere?

17. Which two continents cross the equator?

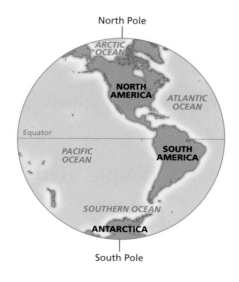

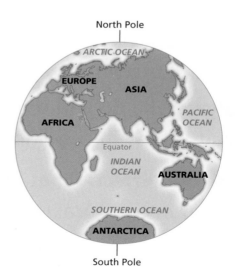

Unit 1 Activities

 ## Unit Writing Activity

Write a Letter Write a letter to a pen pal about a place in or near your community.

■ Think about the place and write a description of it.

■ Include a map that will help your pen pal get around.

 ## Unit Project

Make a Map Design a park and make a map of it.

■ Think of ideas for the design.

■ Show and label landforms and bodies of water.

■ Add a compass rose and a map key.

Read More

■ **Up North and Down South: Using Map Directions** by Doreen Gonzales. Capstone Press, 2008.

■ **The Seven Continents** by Wil Mara. Children's Press, 2005.

■ **The Everything Kid's Geography Book** by Jane P. Gardner and J. Elizabeth Mills. Adams Media, 2009.

Go Digital **Education Place®** visit www.eduplace.com/nycssp/

Unit 2

New York City Over Time

The Big Idea

How and why did New York City change over time?

WHAT TO KNOW

- ✓ Who lived in New York City long ago?
- ✓ Why did settlers come to New York?
- ✓ How did the Erie Canal help New York City grow?
- ✓ How did technology change New York City?
- ✓ What kinds of buildings do people in New York City live in?
- ✓ What kinds of work do people in New York City do?

New York City Transportation

Facts About New York City Subways	
Routes	26
Stations	468
Train Cars	6,400
Miles of track	834

The 7 train goes from Times Square in Manhattan to Flushing, Queens.

NEW JERSEY

The Staten Island ferry runs between Staten Island and Manhattan.

Staten Island

NEW YORK

NEW JERSEY

North
West — East
South

Bronx

Long Island Sound

Hudson River

East River

Manhattan

Port Authority
Bus Terminal

Grand Central Station

LaGuardia Airport

Queens

Penn Station

John F. Kennedy International Airport

Upper New York Bay

Brooklyn

Jamaica Bay

Lower New York Bay

ATLANTIC OCEAN

Map Key

- - - - - Ferry route

Subway lines

Airport

Bus terminal

Train station

57

Reading Social Studies

Cause and Effect

Why It Matters Knowing why things happen can help you understand what you read.

Learn the Skill

■ What makes something happen is a cause.

■ What happens is the effect.

Read the paragraph below.

New York City is not the same as it was long ago. Then, only Native Americans lived on the land that is now the city.

Cause Later, people from Europe came to the area. They needed somewhere

Effect to live. They began to build the city. Over time, many people moved to New York City. They built wider roads, more homes, and taller buildings.

Practice the Skill

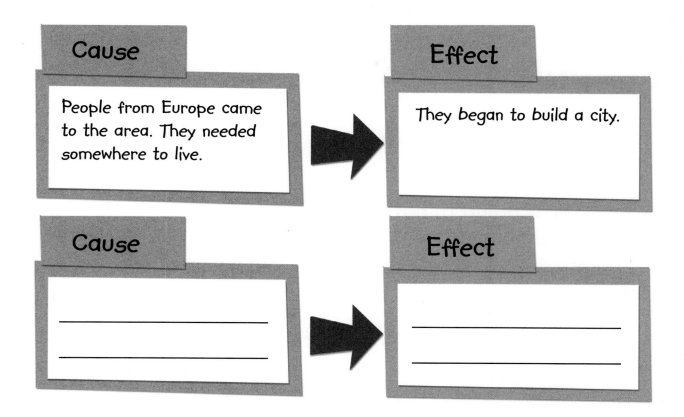

Cause

People from Europe came to the area. They needed somewhere to live.

Effect

They began to build a city.

Cause

_____

_____

Effect

_____

_____

This chart shows what happened in New York City and why it happened. Copy the chart and complete it.

Apply the Skill

As you read this unit, look for ways that New York City has changed. Find out what caused these changes.

Vocabulary Preview

change

New ways of doing things have brought change to New York City. A **change** happens when something becomes different. page 62

explorer

Henry Hudson was an **explorer**. He traveled across the ocean in a ship to find new places. page 66

skyscraper

The Empire State Building is a famous skyscraper in New York City. A **skyscraper** is a very tall building. page 81

culture

Culture is the way of life of a group of people. Celebrations are a part of culture. page 86

 visit www.eduplace.com/nycssp/

61

New York City Long Ago

▶ **What to Know**

Who lived in New York City long ago?

▶ **Vocabulary**

change
history

Reading Skill

Cause and Effect

Before You Read

Think of a time you saw something new in your neighborhood. A new building or park can make a place look different.

Past, Present, and Future

A **change** happens when something becomes different. Many things have changed in New York City over time.

Past

What was New York City like long ago? To find out, you can study the city's history. **History** is everything people can know about what happened long ago.

New York City will continue to change in the future. Workers will build new buildings. New people will move here, and children will grow up. Some day, children will wonder what New York City was like when you were in second grade.

✓**Reading Check** **Cause and Effect** What has caused New York City to change over time?

Present

Native Americans

Hundreds of years ago, many groups of Native Americans lived on the land that is now New York City. They built their villages near bodies of water. They used the natural resources of the area to live. One group was called the Lenape.

They hunted deer, elk, beavers, turkeys, and ducks. They ate clams and oysters from the rivers and bays. They made tools from stones, plants, and bones. They also made shiny beads from shells.

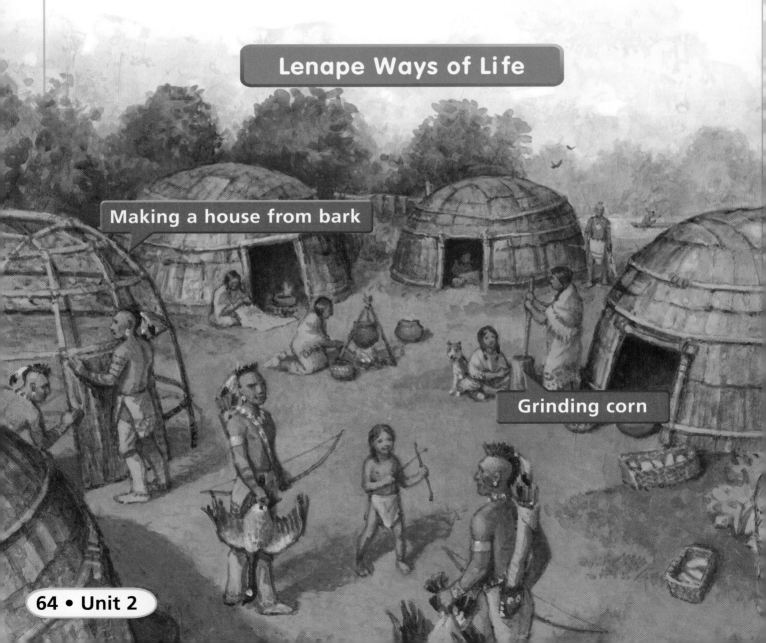

Lenape Ways of Life

Making a house from bark

Grinding corn

Different groups of Native Americans in the area spoke the same language. Canarsie and Rockaway are place names that come from Native American words.

✓ **Reading Check** **Main Idea and Details** What natural resources did Native Americans use?

The Lenape grew crops known as the Three Sisters—corn, beans, and squash.

Growing crops in fields

Lesson Review

❶ **What to Know** Who lived in New York City long ago?

❷ **Vocabulary** Use the word **history** in a sentence.

❸ **Cause and Effect** Why might New York City change in the future?

❹ **Art Activity** Draw pictures of three natural resources the Lenape used long ago.

Lesson 2

Dutch and English in New York

▶ **What to Know**

Why did settlers come to New York?

▶ **Vocabulary**

explorer
settler
colony

Reading Skill

Sequence

Before You Read

Have you ever looked for something and found something else? Sailors looking for a way to Asia found New York Harbor.

Finding New York

More than five hundred years ago, explorers from Europe made journeys to other lands. An **explorer** travels to find new things.

main idea

Henry Hudson's ship was called the Half Moon. This ship is a copy of the Half Moon.

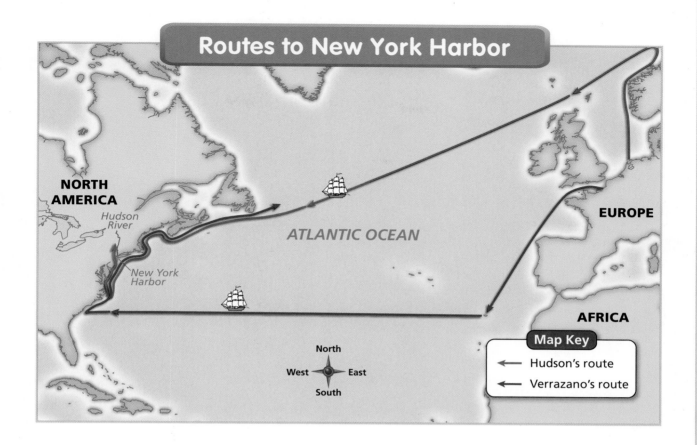

Routes to New York Harbor

NORTH AMERICA

Hudson River

New York Harbor

ATLANTIC OCEAN

EUROPE

AFRICA

North
West — East
South

Map Key
← Hudson's route
← Verrazano's route

In 1492, Christopher Columbus sailed west across the Atlantic Ocean. He was looking for a new way to get to Asia. Instead, he landed in North America.

Giovanni Verrazano sailed into New York Harbor and part way up the Hudson River. The Verrazano Bridge is named for him. Henry Hudson was an explorer who worked for a Dutch company . He sailed further up the Hudson River, which is named for him.

✓ Reading Check **Sequence** Which explorer was the first to sail up the Hudson?

Dutch settlers traded with Europe. Large ships could dock in New Amsterdam's harbor to pick up goods.

Settlers Come to New York

The Dutch started a town called New Amsterdam. Settlers came to live there. A **settler** is a person who makes a home in a new place. The settlers came from many places. They spoke 18 different languages. Some came so they could practice their religion freely. Others traded furs with Native Americans. The furs were used to make hats in Europe.

main idea

England wanted New Amsterdam's harbor because it was good for trade. England took control of New Amsterdam in 1664 and started its own colony. A **colony** is a land ruled by another country. It changed the name of the city to New York.

People in New York kept the Dutch names of some places. Harlem and the Bowery are two names that come from the Dutch language.

New York was named for the Duke of York.

Reading Check Draw Conclusions

Why did England want to take control of New Amsterdam?

Lesson Review

① **What to Know** Why did settlers come to New York?

② **Vocabulary** Use the word **settlers** in a sentence about New Amsterdam.

③ **Sequence** Who settled in New Amsterdam first, the Dutch or the English?

④ **Writing Activity** Write a postcard that an explorer who sailed to New York might have sent back home.

The Growth of New York City

▶ **What to Know**

How did the Erie Canal help New York City grow?

▶ **Vocabulary**

business
immigrant
population
communication

Reading Skill

Cause and Effect

Before You Read

You know that New York is a big city. People came to New York for many reasons.

A Growing City

In 1776, people in the colonies declared independence, or freedom, from England. They fought a war for freedom and became the United States of America. New York was one of America's biggest cities.

Mules pulled barges full of goods down the Erie Canal.

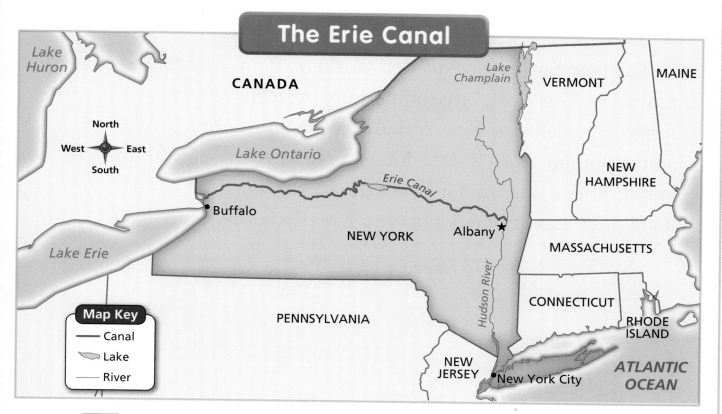

The Erie Canal

Lake Huron

CANADA

Lake Ontario

Lake Champlain

VERMONT

MAINE

NEW HAMPSHIRE

North
West — East
South

Erie Canal

Buffalo

NEW YORK

Albany ★

MASSACHUSETTS

Lake Erie

Hudson River

CONNECTICUT

RHODE ISLAND

Map Key
— Canal
Lake
— River

PENNSYLVANIA

NEW JERSEY

New York City

ATLANTIC OCEAN

Skill **Reading Maps** Which two bodies of water did the Erie Canal connect?

In the early 1800s, New Yorkers built the Erie Canal. Farmers and traders sent goods down the canal and the Hudson River to New York City. Ships carried goods from New York Harbor to other cities and countries.

main idea

New York City became a business center. **Business** is the making or selling of goods and services. New shops and businesses opened. Many people came to New York City to work. New York became the biggest city in the United States.

✓ Reading Check **Cause and Effect** Why did the Erie Canal cause New York City to grow?

A Business Center

The new businesses needed workers. People moved to New York City to find jobs. African Americans came to New York City from southern states. People from Puerto Rico came, too. Immigrants came from all over the world. An **immigrant** leaves one country to live in another one.

Resources Used in New York City	
Resource	**Uses**
	to make bread
	to make clothing
	to build houses and ships
	for fishing, shipping, and trade

Skill **Reading Charts** What was lumber used for?

A worker cans oysters gathered in New York Bay.

Life in a New York City neighborhood

As more immigrants came, the population of New York City grew. **Population** is the number of people who live in a place. Immigrants settled near others who spoke the same language, ate the same food, and had the same traditions. People from Italy lived near others who spoke Italian. Their neighborhood was called Little Italy. People from China lived near restaurants and stores that sold Chinese food. Their neighborhood was called Chinatown.

main ★ idea

Reading Check **Problem and Solution** How did immigrants solve the problems of living in a new country?

Modern New York City

New York City has changed and grown in many ways during the last 100 years. Growing businesses brought money to New York City. Many banks opened. New York became the center for business and banking in the United States.

Businesses wanted to be able to send news quickly. The sharing of news and information is called **communication**. Telephones and newspapers are two kinds of communication. Many newspapers and magazines are made in New York City.

New York City was the first place to use telephones. Switchboard operators made sure calls went to the right place.

Television is another way to share news. Many TV studios are located in New York City.

People who made money in business opened museums and theaters. Painters, writers, and actors came to the city. It became a center for the arts.

Reading Check Categorize What are two types of businesses that grew in modern New York City?

Lesson Review

❶ **What to Know** How did the Erie Canal help New York City grow?

❷ **Vocabulary** Use the word **communication** in a sentence about something you use now.

❸ **Cause and Effect** Why did people move to New York City from other places?

❹ **Writing Activity** Write a letter an immigrant might have written to family in his or her home country.

Frederick Law Olmsted

Frederick Law Olmsted designed many of our country's famous parks. He wanted people in cities to enjoy nature. In 1857, New York City held a contest for a design for Central Park. Olmsted worked on a plan with Calvert Vaux, another park designer. Their design had walking paths, trails for horses, and roads for carriages. Their plan won.

Olmsted organized the work of building the park. About 4,000 workers did the job. A few years later, Olmsted and Vaux planned Prospect Park in Brooklyn. Olmsted designed parks where the city's people could come together to relax and play.

Today, visitors to Central Park can go boating, rock climbing, and ice skating. They can go to the zoo or see a play.

Workers built the Music Pavillion to hold concerts.

Activities

1. **Think About It** In what ways did Frederick Law Olmsted show he cared about the people of New York City?

2. **Draw It** Draw something you like to add to your favorite park.

Use a Timeline

A timeline can show events in history. A **timeline** is an ordered group of words and dates that shows when events happened. Look at this timeline of New York's history.

▶ **Vocabulary**

timeline

Learn the Skill

Step 1 The title tells what the timeline is about. The timeline has a line divided into equal parts. Each part stands for a century, or 100 years.

Step 2 Look at the numbers on the timeline. The numbers are years. You read a timeline from left to right. The earliest numbers and events are on the left.

Step 3 The numbers with the events on the timeline tell the year in which the event happened.

1600   1700

1609
Henry Hudson explored what is now New York.

Use the timeline to answer the questions below.

1 What happened in 1789?

2 Was the Erie Canal opened before or after Henry Hudson explored what is now New York?

3 In what year was the Empire State Building built?

American History

1800   1900   2000

1789
George Washington became the first President of the United States.

1825
The Erie Canal opened.

1931
The Empire State Building was built.

Apply the Skill

Make a timeline of important events in your life.

Technology and Change

▶ **What to Know**

How did technology change New York City?

▶ **Vocabulary**

technology
elevator
skyscraper

Reading Skill

Main Idea and Details

Before You Read

What is the tallest building you've ever seen? Before the 1880s, few buildings had more than five or six floors.

Taller and Bigger

New technology gave people a way to build tall buildings. **Technology** is using science to make things work better. People found out how to build strong steel bars to keep tall buildings up. They learned to make **elevators** to go to high floors.

main idea

The first skyscraper was 11 floors, or stories, high. People called a tall building a **skyscraper** because it reached so high. The next tallest building was 21 stories.

In 1931, the Empire State Building was built. It had more than 100 stories. It was the tallest building in the world for more than 40 years. Today, it is still a symbol of New York City.

✓ Reading Check **Main Idea and Details** What new technology was used to build skyscrapers?

Skill **Reading Graphs** Which building is 77 stories tall?

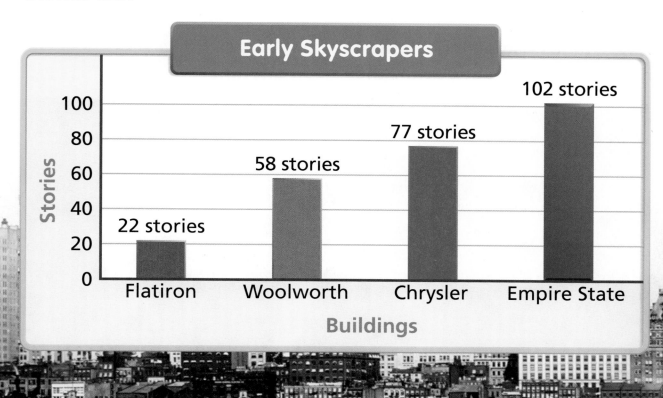

Early Skyscrapers

Stories

- 22 stories — Flatiron
- 58 stories — Woolworth
- 77 stories — Chrysler
- 102 stories — Empire State

Buildings

Brighter and Faster

Electricity came to New York City in the 1880s. Trains used electricity to move through tunnels underground. The trains were called subways. New York City's first subway was built more than 100 years ago. Electric lights made streets safer at night. People in houses could read books. Stores could stay open after dark.

In the 1950s, many families bought televisions. TVs run on electricity.

Newsstands use electric lights to stay open all night. People can buy what they need anytime.

This train runs under the ground in some places and above the ground in others.

Subways were faster than streetcars or trams. People who used subways could live farther away from their jobs. They moved to Harlem, Washington Heights, Brooklyn, Queens, and the Bronx.

✓ **Reading Check** Cause and Effect How did electricity change daily life?

Lesson Review

❶ **What to Know** How did technology change New York City?

❷ **Vocabulary** Write a sentence about the first **skyscrapers**.

❸ **Main Idea and Details** Write two details about the Empire State Building.

❹ **Art Activity** Make a bulletin board to show ways you use electricity. Draw pictures and write sentences to explain what your pictures show.

People and Neighborhoods of New York City

What to Know

What kinds of buildings do people in New York City live in?

Vocabulary

apartment
culture

Reading Skill

Compare and Contrast

New York has many neighborhoods. Each neighborhood is different from the others.

main idea

Many families live in this apartment building in Brooklyn.

Settling in the City

Some neighborhoods have tall buildings with apartments. An **apartment** is one or more rooms used as a place to live in a larger building. Other neighborhoods have smaller houses.

✓ **Reading Check** **Compare and Contrast** How are the apartment building and the small house alike?

One family lives in this New York City house.

People can express culture through music. Many famous musicians have played at the Apollo Theater in Harlem.

A City of Neighbors

Neighborhoods are made up of people from different cultures. A **culture** is a group's way of life. Language, food, clothing, and traditions are all part of a group's culture.

main idea

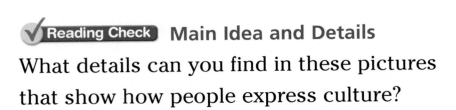

✓ Reading Check **Main Idea and Details**

What details can you find in these pictures that show how people express culture?

In Chinatown, a group of men play Chinese chess, a traditional game.

People in Little Italy have many festivals with traditional food and music to celebrate their culture.

main idea

Living Together

The history and geography of New York City make it a special place. People have moved to the city for hundreds of years. They come from many countries and bring their culture with them.

Today, New York City's neighborhoods have diversity, or different ideas and ways of living. People who live in New York enjoy learning about many cultures. The St. Patrick's Day parade and Chinese New Year are two celebrations that show the diversity of the city's culture.

✓ **Reading Check** **Draw Conclusions**

Do you think the cultures in New York City are the same as cultures of other cities? Why or why not?

❶ What to Know

What kinds of buildings do people in New York City live in?

❷ Compare and Contrast

How are the neighborhoods of New York City alike and different?

❸ Case Study Detective

Would you expect to find something like this near the front door of an apartment building or a house? Explain your answer.

❹ Word Play

Unscramble the letters to find things that are part of culture.

dofo _____

locitnhg _____

lavsfetis _____

eglaguan _____

Immigrants at Ellis Island

Where did immigrants go after their ships passed the Statue of Liberty? Most went to Ellis Island. There, inspectors asked immigrants questions. "Where did you come from? Can you read and write? Do you have a job waiting for you?"

Each immigrant was checked by a doctor. People who were sick had to stay on the island until they were well again. They were given food and drinks. Children played games, went to school, and started learning about their new country. When they got better, immigrants could leave the island to start new lives in America.

Ellis Island was built to keep track of the millions of immigrants coming to America from other countries.

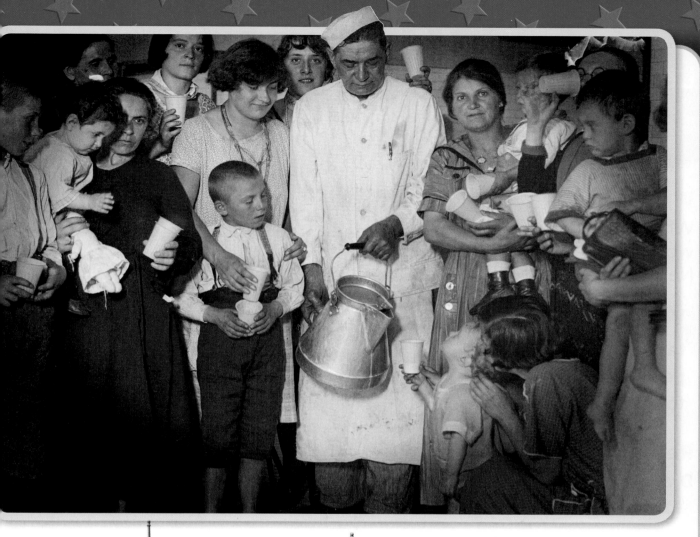

Women and children at Ellis Island were given snacks.

Activities

1. **Act It Out** Role-play arriving at Ellis Island. Think about what might have happened there.

2. **Write About It** Describe what is happening in the photograph on this page.

 Go Digital Visit Education Place for more primary sources. www.eduplace.com/nycssp/

Lesson 6

▶ What to Know

What kinds of work do people in New York City do?

▶ Vocabulary

factory
performer
tourism

◉ Reading Skill

Draw Conclusions

Working and Living in New York City

New Yorkers have different jobs. Some make goods. Other provide services.

Working in New York City

Some people make things in a factory. A **factory** is a building in which people use machines to make goods.

People who work in office buildings might work on computers, answer phones, and go to meetings.

Other workers have jobs that help or serve people. These jobs are called service jobs. Workers in a bank serve their customers. Food servers bring food to you and your family in a restaurant.

✓ **Reading Check** **Draw Conclusions**

What do you think people who work in a factory might need to learn?

> Some New Yorkers are performers. Performers dance, act, or make music.

> Taxi drivers help their riders get where they need to go.

93

Fun in New York City

Many people live and work in New York City. Millions of visitors come to visit and have fun.

Many jobs in New York City are in tourism. **Tourism** is the business of helping visitors. People who work in hotels, sell tickets, and lead tours of famous places work in tourism.

main ★ idea

A lot of tourists visit the Bronx Zoo. So do a lot of people who live in New York.

✓ **Reading Check** **Categorize** What kind of business do people who lead tours of the Statue of Liberty work in?

Facts About the
Bronx Zoo

- More than 100 years old
- More than 2 million visitors each year
- More than 6,000 animals
- More than 750 workers

Skill **Reading Visuals** What kinds of animals can you spot in this picture?

Learning in New York City

Going to the zoo is fun. It is also a great way to learn. Another fun place for learning is the American Museum of Natural History. Tourists agree! Many people from other cities come to New York City to see this museum.

main idea ⭐

✓ **Reading Check** **Cause and Effect** Why would tourists visit a zoo or museum?

CASE STUDY REVIEW

❶ What to Know

What kinds of work do people in New York City do?

❷ Draw Conclusions

Why do many people in New York City work in tourism?

❸ Case Study Detective

Where can you see this famous lion? Hint: You can find lots of books inside this building. You will also find DVDs and computers.

❹ Word Play

Take letters from the Letter Bank. Use them to fill in the blanks and find the things tourists might do in New York.

_____hop

visit _____useums

see _____hows

hear musi_____

ea_____

Letter Bank
C M S S T

New York City's Heritage

Heritage is traditions and values passed on by people who lived before us. You can see the heritage of New York City everywhere you look. It is in the streets and buildings around you.

Carnegie Hall is known for great music. Many famous performers have played here.

People started building the Cathedral of St. John the Divine more than 100 years ago. They wanted a church for all the people of New York.

France gave the Statue of Liberty to the United States. It is a symbol of freedom. It welcomed many immigrants to America.

An old wall once stood along Wall Street. Today many banks and other important businesses are located there.

Activities

1. **Talk About It** Why is the Statue of Liberty an important symbol?

2. **Present It** Make a poster about a street or building that shows New York City heritage. Explain why this place is important.

Order, Please

List the events in order in your notebook. Start with the earliest event.

Electricity comes to New York.

The Empire State Building is built.

Only Native Americans live in New York.

People today celebrate culture.

Explorers sail into New York Harbor.

The Erie Canal Opens.

Word Fun

Answer the questions.

Do immigrants to the United States add to or subtract from its population?

What does a skyscraper need most—a factory, an elevator, or a performer?

Who comes first, an explorer or a settler?

Answer the riddle

Where do both settlers and ants live?

Review for Understanding

Reading Social Studies

What makes something happen is a **cause**.
What happens is the **effect**.

Cause and Effect

1. Complete the graphic organizer to show that you understand the relationship between cause and effect.

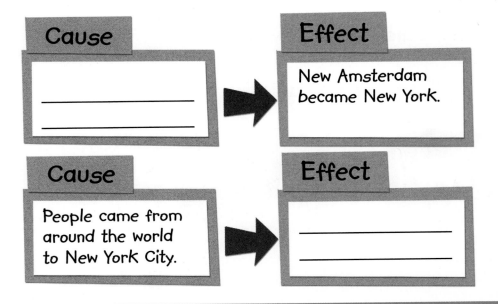

Cause		Effect
_____ _____	→	New Amsterdam became New York.
Cause People came from around the world to New York City.	→	**Effect** _____ _____

The Big Idea Write About the Big Idea

2. **Write a Story** People and places change over time. Write a story that describes how a person or place you know has changed over time.

Vocabulary

Choose the letter of the correct word.

3. A group's way of life

4. A person who travels to find new things

5. The business of helping visitors

6. A very tall building

7. When something becomes different

A. **change** (page 62)

B. **explorer** (page 66)

C. **skyscraper** (page 81)

D. **culture** (page 86)

E. **tourism** (page 94)

Facts and Main Ideas

Write a sentence to answer each question.

8. Which two explorers visited the area that is now New York City?

9. Who took over New Amsterdam from the Dutch?

10. Why did New Yorkers build the Erie Canal?

11. What helped people to build taller buildings?

12. How did electricity affect how people lived in New York City?

Critical Thinking

Write a short answer for each question.

13. Cause and Effect What are some of the things that have affected culture in New York City?

14. Draw Conclusions Why might people want to visit New York City?

Skillbuilders   Use a Timeline

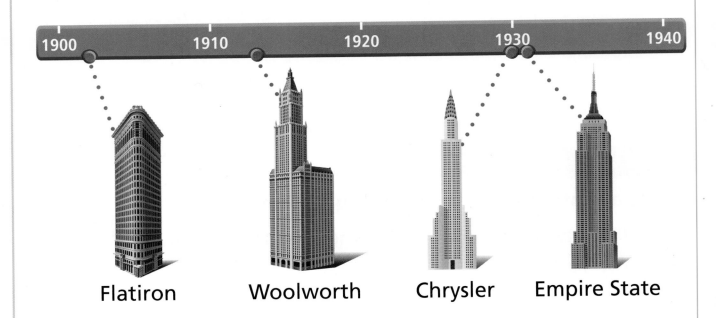

Flatiron   Woolworth   Chrysler   Empire State

15. What is the first date on the timeline? Last date?

16. Which skyscraper was built in 1913?

17. Was the Chrysler Building built before or after the Empire State Building?

18. How many years after the Flatiron Building was finished was the Chrysler Building built?

Unit 2 Activities

 ## Unit Writing Activity

Write a Narrative Think about your past and present. What events do you want to share?

- Write a paragraph about the events.
- Put the events in order on a timeline.

 ## Unit Project

Storyboard Design a family history storyboard.

- Interview family members.
- Collect photographs or draw pictures of events.
- Put the pictures in order. Share the storyboard.

Read More

- **Ellis Island** by Elaine Landau. Children's Press, 2008.
- **Skyscraper** by Susan E. Goodman and Michael Doolittle. Knopf Books for Young Readers, 2004.
- **Henry Hudson: Discoverer of the Hudson River** by Jeff C. Young. Enslow Publishers, 2009.

Go Digital **Education Place®** visit www.eduplace.com/nycssp/

Unit 3

Urban, Suburban, and Rural Communities

The Big Idea

Why and how do communities develop differently?

What to Know

- ✔ What are some reasons people choose to live in a place?
- ✔ What kinds of communities do people live in?
- ✔ What is life like in a suburb?
- ✔ What is life like in a rural area?

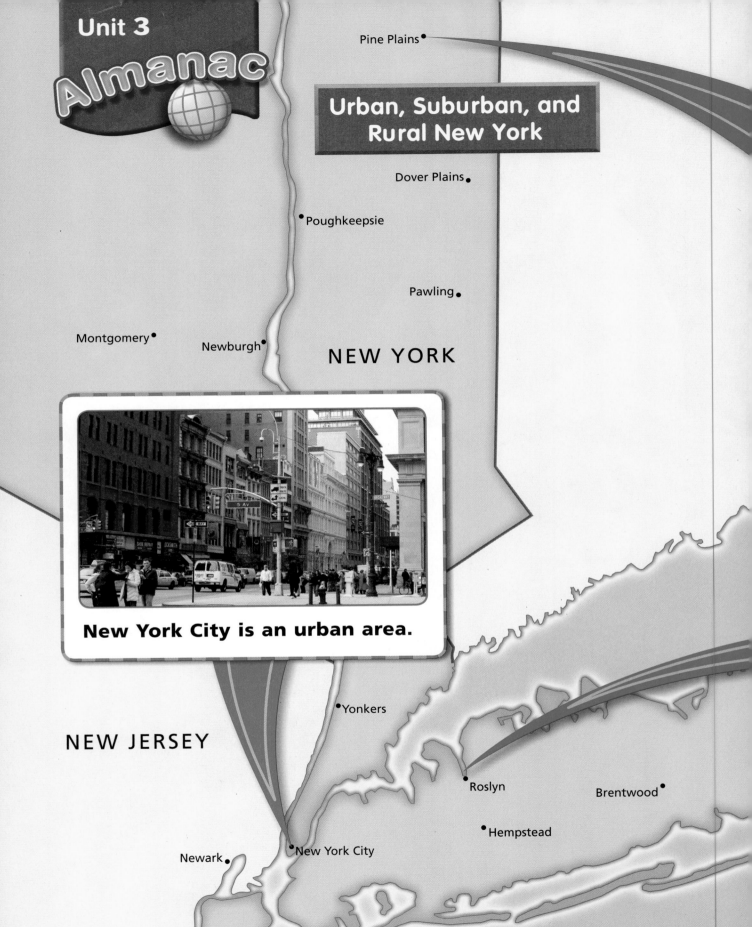

Almanac

Urban, Suburban, and Rural New York

Pine Plains•

Dover Plains•

•Poughkeepsie

Pawling•

Montgomery•

Newburgh•

NEW YORK

New York City is an urban area.

•Yonkers

NEW JERSEY

Roslyn•

Brentwood•

•Hempstead

Newark•   •New York City

.Hartford

CONNECTICUT

RHODE ISLAND

Pine Plains is a rural area.

Long Island Sound

North

West ✦ East

South

•Sag Harbor

Hampton Bays•

Roslyn is a suburb.

ATLANTIC OCEAN

Map Key

• City

— State boundary

Reading Social Studies

Compare and Contrast

Why It Matters Thinking about how some things are alike and different can help you understand what you read.

Learn the Skill

■ To compare, think about how people, places, or things are the same.

■ To contrast, think about how people, places, or things are different.

Read the paragraph below.

Compare Asheville, North Carolina, and New York City are two cities in the United States.

Contrast Visitors to Asheville can hike in the mountains or go fishing. New York City is a good place to visit museums and historic places. Visitors to both cities can shop for gifts.

Asheville

New York City

Practice the Skill

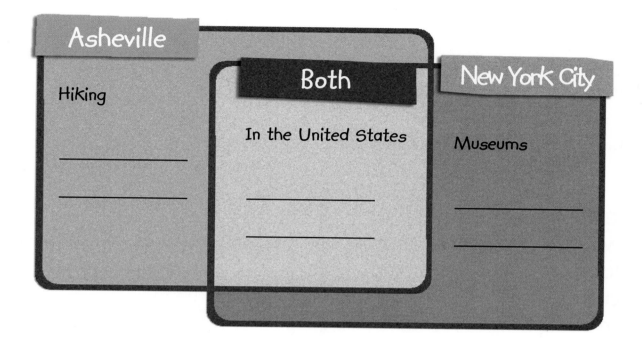

Asheville

Hiking

_____

_____

Both

In the United States

_____

_____

New York City

Museums

_____

_____

This chart shows how these two cities are the same and how they are different. What can you add to the chart? Copy the chart and complete it.

Apply the Skill

As you read this unit, look for ways to compare and contrast places where people live.

Vocabulary Preview

climate

Climate is the kind of weather a place has over a long time. People in cold climates can play in the snow in winter. page 116

urban area

An **urban area** is a place where many people live and work close together.

page 120

suburb

Some people live in suburbs. A **suburb** is a community near a city. page 121

rural area

A **rural area** has more open space than a suburb or an urban area. page 122

Go Digital visit www.eduplace.com/nycssp/

People Live Together

▶ **What to Know**
What are some reasons people choose to live in a place?

▶ **Vocabulary**
shelter
climate

Reading Skill
Compare and Contrast

Before You Read

What natural resources are near your community? They may have affected how the community grew.

Where People Live

When people start a new community, they first choose where to settle. They may look at the geography of a place. Natural resources can affect where people start a community.

main idea

All people need food, water, and shelter. A **shelter** is something that protects or covers. In some places, these things are hard to get. In dry deserts and rocky mountains, it is hard to find water or grow food. People may not choose to live there.

Other places have flat land and rich soil that are good for growing food. They have rivers for water and fish. Areas that have lots of natural resources might grow faster than areas that do not.

✔ Reading Check **Compare and Contrast** Are people more likely to settle near rich soil or in a desert?

Water and mountains are natural resources near Lake Placid, New York. People who like to swim, sail, and ski visit Lake Placid.

How People Live

Climate affects how people live. **Climate** is the kind of weather a place has over a long time. Some people live in areas with cold winters. Builders there need to plan schools and other buildings to be warm in winter. Other people live in warm places. Buildings in those places might need to stay cool all year.

Skill **Reading Visuals** What details in the photo tell you that this is a warm climate?

Do you like playing in the snow? People in cold climates also have to shovel snow to clear sidewalks and driveways.

Places with cold climates may have indoor areas to play sports in winter. They might also have tunnels and skyways so that people can move from place to place easily during blizzards. Buildings in places with strong storms must be sturdy enough to keep people safe.

Reading Check **Main Idea and Details** What kind of buildings do places that have storms need?

Lesson Review

1 **What to Know** What are some reasons people choose to live in a place?

2 **Vocabulary** Write one or two sentences about the **climate** where you live.

3 **Compare and Contrast** In what kind of climate might children play sports indoors in winter?

4 **Art Activity** Draw a picture of one way climate affects how you live.

Study Skills

Skillbuilder

Use Reference Materials

▶ **Vocabulary**

dictionary
encyclopedia
Internet

You can find out more about a topic by using reference materials.

Learn the Skill

A **dictionary** is a book that tells what words mean. An **encyclopedia** is a set of books that has articles on different topics. Reference materials can be found on the Internet. The **Internet** is a large system of connected computers.

Step 1 The information in reference books is often in ABC order. To find the word **roof** in a dictionary, look in the section that begins with the letter R. To find the article titled **roof** in an encyclopedia, look in the book labeled with the letter R.

Step 2 After you find the R section, you need to find the right page. The **guidewords** can help you. They show the first and last word of each page.

Step 3 Use ABC order to find the word **roof**.

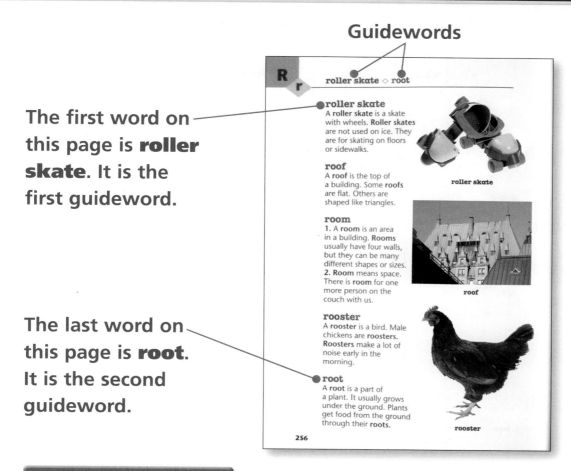

Guidewords

roller skate ◇ root

R r

roller skate
A **roller skate** is a skate with wheels. **Roller skates** are not used on ice. They are for skating on floors or sidewalks.

roof
A **roof** is the top of a building. Some **roofs** are flat. Others are shaped like triangles.

room
1. A **room** is an area in a building. **Rooms** usually have four walls, but they can be many different shapes or sizes. 2. **Room** means space. There is **room** for one more person on the couch with us.

rooster
A **rooster** is a bird. Male chickens are **roosters**. **Roosters** make a lot of noise early in the morning.

root
A **root** is a part of a plant. It usually grows under the ground. Plants get food from the ground through their **roots**.

roller skate

roof

rooster

256

The first word on this page is **roller skate**. It is the first guideword.

The last word on this page is **root**. It is the second guideword.

Practice the Skill

Follow the directions.

1 Use a dictionary to find the definitions of these words: **community, climate, location**

2 Tell which reference materials you might use to find out how climate affects communities.

Apply the Skill

Use two different reference materials to look up a topic you would like to research.

Large and Small Communities

▶ **What to Know**
What kinds of communities do people live in?

▶ **Vocabulary**
urban area
suburb
rural area

Reading Skill
Cause and Effect

Before You Read

Does your community have houses with big yards? Or do you live where buildings are close together?

Urban Areas

Communities can be different sizes. New York City is a large city. Another name for city is **urban area**. Many people live and work in urban areas. Cars, buses, and trucks fill the streets. Buildings are close together in cities. People can walk to stores. They can hear concerts and go to plays. Children can play in city parks.

main ★ idea

A busy street in New York City

A suburban street in Radburn, New Jersey

Suburbs

A **suburb** is a smaller community near a city. Homes in suburbs are farther apart than buildings in cities. Most homes have yards. People have to drive to stores and other places. Radburn, New Jersey, is a suburb near New York City. Not as many people live in Radburn as in New York City.

✓ Reading Check **Cause and Effect** What is one effect of places being farther apart in Radburn?

Rural Areas

Outside of cities and suburbs are rural areas. **Rural areas** are places in the country with more open space than cities and suburbs. Sharon Springs is a rural area in New York State. It has fewer stores, schools, and homes than New York City or Radburn. Most farms are in rural areas. Farmers need a lot of land to grow crops. Many people in rural areas sell what they grow or make to people in other communities.

main idea

A farm in Sharon Springs, New York

Moving Between Communities

People have different reasons for moving to a community. People who want to live in a large home near a city might move to a suburb. Those who want open space and a large garden might move to a rural area. People who enjoy being around other people and going to concerts might move to an urban area.

main idea

Reading Check Main Idea and Details What areas have the most farms?

Cities, Suburbs, and Farms

Skill **Reading Maps** How might people in Radburn get to New York City?

Lesson Review

❶ **What to Know** What kinds of communities do people live in?

❷ **Vocabulary** Write a sentence that tells two ways that an **urban area** is different from a **suburb**.

❸ **Cause and Effect** What might cause an urban area to have more things to do than a rural area?

❹ **Art Activity** Draw pictures of things you might find in a rural area that you would not find in a city or suburb.

Majora Carter

What makes a person proud of her community? Majora Carter decided it was beautiful, healthy neighborhoods. Carter grew up in the South Bronx. She wanted to make her community a better, healthier place to live.

Majora Carter started a group that works in the South Bronx. Her projects have built paths for walking and bicycling near the Bronx River. She worked to get rid of pollution in the community. Carter also started programs to train people for better jobs. She has won many awards for her work. Now Carter helps communities around the country.

Carter's group helped build Hunts Point Riverside Park. People can enjoy nature or attend community events in the park.

Activities

1. **Discuss It** What did Majora Carter do to help her community?

2. **Write About It** Write about a project children could do to make your school a better place.

Skillbuilder

Compare Fact and Opinion

▶ **Vocabulary**

fact
opinion

A **fact** is something that is true. An **opinion** is what someone thinks. Two people can have different opinions about the same facts.

Learn the Skill

Step 1 Read the sentences about communities. One sentence tells a fact. The other sentence tells an opinion.

Step 2 A fact is something that is true. You can check to see if a fact is true. A fact is probably true if two or more good nonfiction books agree on it.

Step 3 Opinions use words such as "I think."

Cities have more people than rural areas.

I think a rural community is the best place to live.

Read the sentences below. Then follow the directions.

1 In what way is a fact different from an opinion?

2 Which sentences tell facts?

3 Which sentence tells an opinion? Tell how you know that it is an opinion.

Suburbs are communities near cities.

I think living in New York City is fun.

New York City is a large community.

Apply the Skill

Write one fact and one opinion about the community where you live.

A Suburban Community

▶ **What to Know**
What is life like in a suburb?

▶ **Vocabulary**
commute

Reading Skill
Main Idea and Details

Suburbs are different from cities or rural areas. They have special features.

Growing Suburbs

Madison, Connecticut, is a suburb of New Haven. Madison has homes and small businesses. Many people have moved to suburbs like Madison. Their populations are growing.

Children in Madison, Connecticut, have room to play in their yards.

Homes in Suburbs

Suburbs have more space, fewer apartment buildings, and larger homes than cities. Homes in Madison have more land than homes in New Haven. Many have yards with swing sets or gardens. Homes in suburbs are grouped in neighborhoods. Children who live in the same neighborhood might play together and go to the same school.

main idea ★

✓ **Reading Check** **Main Idea and Details** What are some features of homes in suburbs?

Madison

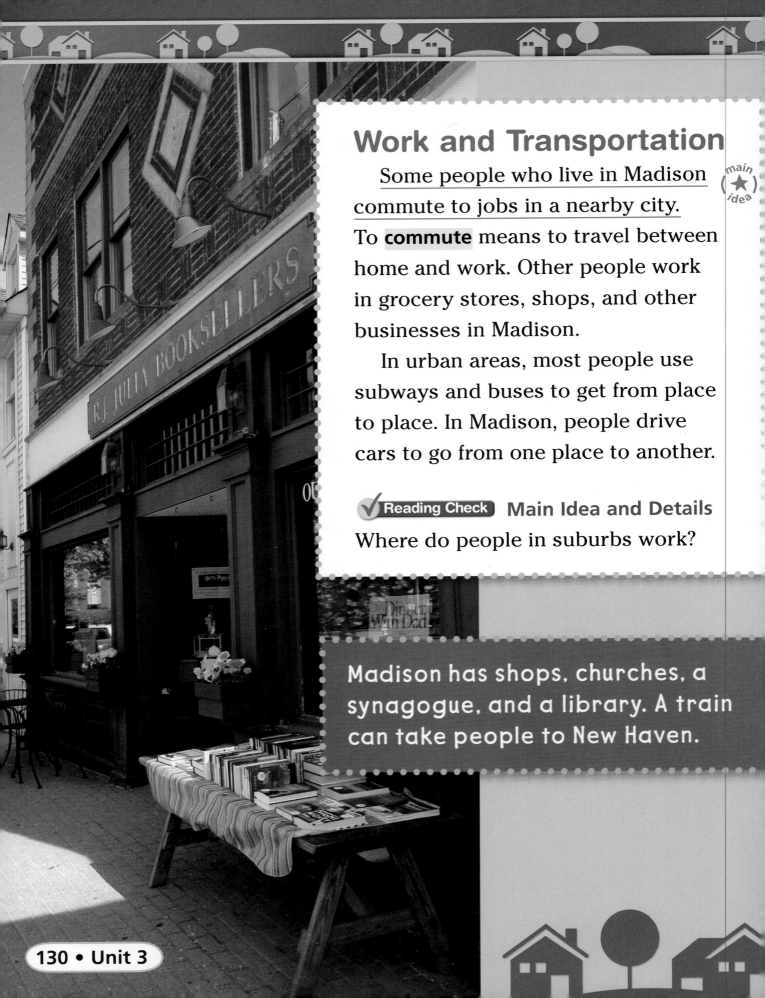

Work and Transportation

Some people who live in Madison commute to jobs in a nearby city. To **commute** means to travel between home and work. Other people work in grocery stores, shops, and other businesses in Madison.

In urban areas, most people use subways and buses to get from place to place. In Madison, people drive cars to go from one place to another.

✓ Reading Check Main Idea and Details

Where do people in suburbs work?

Madison has shops, churches, a synagogue, and a library. A train can take people to New Haven.

Downtown Madison

Map Key
- 🏛 Church
- 📖 Library
- 🛍 Shopping
- 🚈 Train Station

Bradley Road

Wall Street

Durham Road

Tuxis Pond

Madison Green

Boston Post Road

Madison Historic District

North
West — East
South

Skill **Reading Maps**

What is north of the library?

Benefits and Challenges

There are benefits and challenges to living in suburbs. People who live in suburbs have more space than those who live in cities. Suburban neighborhoods are quieter than urban areas. People who live in suburbs can visit the city to have fun.

Living in suburbs has challenges, too. There are not as many places to work or things to do. Workers who commute may have long drives or train rides.

main idea

✓ **Reading Check** **Cause and Effect** What is one challenge of living in the suburbs?

Families in suburbs might have swings in their back yards.

CASE STUDY REVIEW

❶ What to Know

What is life like in a suburb?

❷ Main Idea and Details

List three details about work in a suburb.

❸ Case Study Detective

Which kind of transportation are people who live in the suburbs most likely to use?

❹ Word Play

Unscramble these words about suburbs.

bnoeoighhdor _____

ophs _____

mcemuot _____

aydr _____

Levittown

Many people want to own a home, but homes cost a lot of money. Levittown was built so more people could own homes. This famous suburb of New York City was started more than 60 years ago. Builders wanted to make houses that did not cost very much. To save money, they made all of the houses very similar. Levittown was a big success. Families rushed to buy the low-cost houses. In two years, more than 17,000 houses were built in Levittown.

Families could buy a home in Levittown for less than $8,000.

Most of the houses in Levittown were built to look the same.

Activities

1. **Talk About It** Look at the two photographs of Levittown. Talk about what you see.

2. **Compare It** Write about how the suburb of Levittown is the same as and different from where you live.

 Visit Education Place for more primary sources. www.eduplace.com/nycssp/

Lesson 4

What to Know
What is life like in a rural area?

Vocabulary
farming

Reading Skill
Draw Conclusions

A Rural Community

In rural areas, there are not as many people as in suburbs. People in rural areas may live in small towns. The towns are often far apart.

main idea

Life in a Rural Town

Traer is a rural town in Iowa. It is far away from the nearest large city, Cedar Rapids. People's homes are far apart. They might have to drive to visit their neighbors. Rural areas do not have trains and buses as cities do.

✔ **Reading Check** **Draw Conclusions** Why are people's homes far apart in rural areas?

Fewer than 2,000 people live in Traer, Iowa.

Plants and Animals

Many rural businesses use the natural resources of the area around them. Farmers use soil and water to grow food on farms. Farming is an important business in Traer. **Farming** means growing crops or raising animals. Rural areas have more kinds of plants and animals than suburbs or cities.

main idea

✓ **Reading Check** Classify What is one important business in rural areas?

Farmers in Traer raise cows, pigs, and horses. These animals need a lot of space.

Farmers use tractors to plow, plant seeds, rake, and move things.

People in rural areas may work where they live. Farmers often live on their farms.

The corn grown in Traer is used to make cereal and other products. The products are sold in cities and suburbs around the country.

Benefits and Challenges

There are benefits and challenges to living in rural areas. People in rural areas can have fun outdoors. In Iowa, people use skis, tubes, and boards to play in the snow. In summer, they play golf and baseball and enjoy lakes and rivers.

People in rural areas face challenges as well. Hospitals, police, and firefighters may be far from houses. There are few buses or trains, and travel to a large city may take a long time.

main idea

✓ **Reading Check** **Main Idea and Details** What is one benefit of living in a rural community?

Visitors to Traer can ride in a hot air balloon.

❶ What to Know

What is life like in a rural area?

❷ Draw Conclusions

Why is farming an important business in rural areas?

❸ Case Study Detective

Do you think this lawn mower would most likely be used in a suburb or rural area? Why?

❹ Word Play

Use the following clues to figure out the mystery word.

• important business in rural areas
• growing crops or raising animals
• uses natural resources such as soil and water

__ A __ MI __ G

New York State Festivals

The apple is New York's state fruit. New York City is nicknamed The Big Apple.

Let's celebrate! Communities around New York State hold festivals each year. Some towns celebrate music or dance. Others celebrate harvests of local crops. Races, rides, concerts, art shows, and special foods bring people to the festivals. Everyone in the community can enjoy these events.

The largest pumpkin ever grown in New York was more than 1,600 pounds!

July is the peak of blueberry harvest season in New York and across the United States.

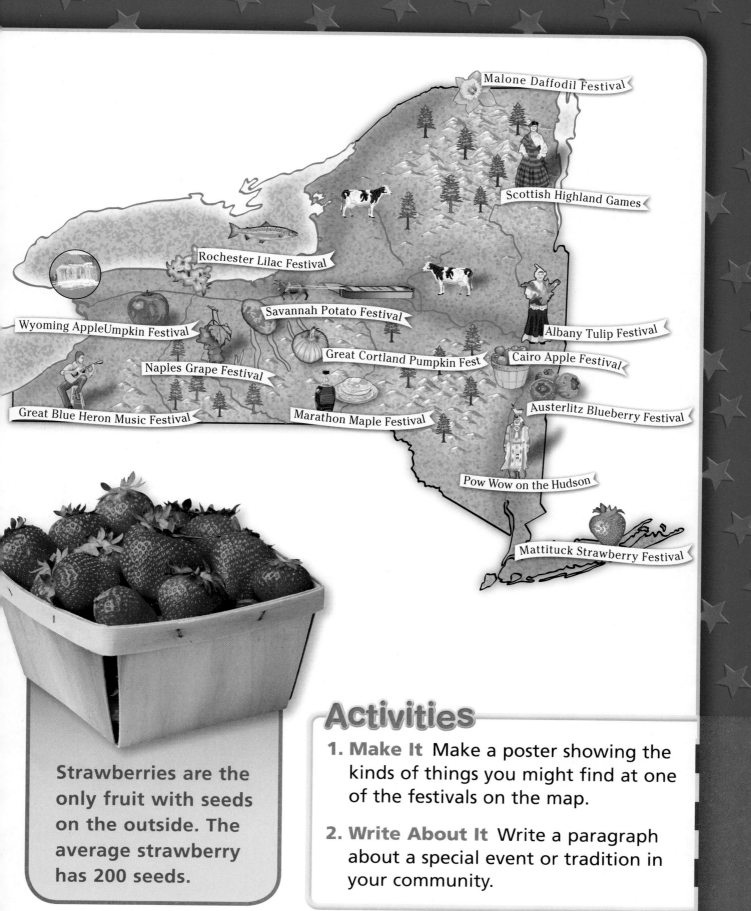

Malone Daffodil Festival

Scottish Highland Games

Rochester Lilac Festival

Wyoming AppleUmpkin Festival

Savannah Potato Festival

Albany Tulip Festival

Great Cortland Pumpkin Fest

Cairo Apple Festival

Naples Grape Festival

Great Blue Heron Music Festival

Marathon Maple Festival

Austerlitz Blueberry Festival

Pow Wow on the Hudson

Mattituck Strawberry Festival

Strawberries are the only fruit with seeds on the outside. The average strawberry has 200 seeds.

Activities

1. **Make It** Make a poster showing the kinds of things you might find at one of the festivals on the map.

2. **Write About It** Write a paragraph about a special event or tradition in your community.

What Doesn't Belong?

Look at the picture of an urban area. Find seven things that belong in a rural area.

STORE

Reading Social Studies

Thinking about how things are alike and different can help you understand what you read.

 Compare and Contrast

1. Complete the graphic organizer to show that you understand how things are alike and different.

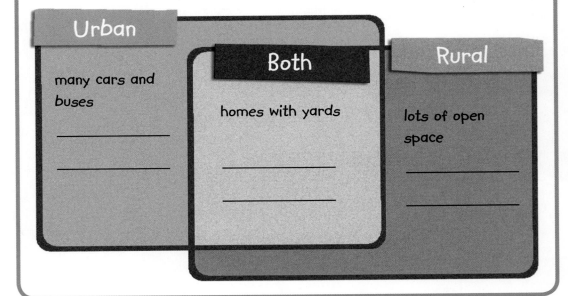

Urban

many cars and buses

_____

_____

Both

homes with yards

_____

_____

Rural

lots of open space

_____

_____

★ **Write About the Big Idea**

2. **Write a Paragraph** Communities develop differently. Write a paragraph to tell two ways urban and rural communities are different.

Vocabulary

Complete each sentence.

3. New York City is an _____.

4. Most farms can be found in a _____.

5. A _____ is a smaller community near a city.

6. Some people _____ into the city to work.

7. Cold winters are part of New York City's _____.

> A. **climate** (page 116)
>
> B. **urban area** (page 120)
>
> C. **suburb** (page 121)
>
> D. **rural area** (page 122)
>
> E. **commute** (page 130)

Facts and Main Ideas

Write a sentence to answer each question.

8. How do natural resources affect where people settle?

9. What kinds of transportation do people in urban areas use? People in suburbs?

Critical Thinking

Write a short answer for each question.

10. **Compare and Contrast** In what ways are urban areas and suburbs alike?

11. **Analyze** How do geography and climate affect the way people live?

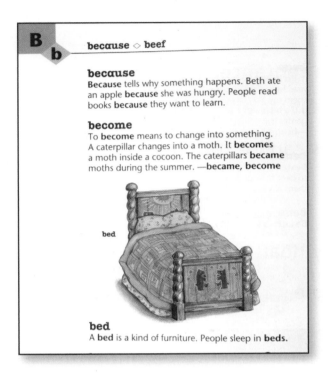

because ◇ beef

because
Because tells why something happens. Beth ate an apple **because** she was hungry. People read books **because** they want to learn.

become
To **become** means to change into something. A caterpillar changes into a moth. It **becomes** a moth inside a cocoon. The caterpillars **became** moths during the summer. —**became, become**

bed

bed
A **bed** is a kind of furniture. People sleep in **beds**.

12. What is the first guideword on the dictionary page?

13. What is the definition of **because**?

Compare Fact and Opinion

A fact is something that is true. An opinion is what someone thinks.

14. Which sentence tells a fact?

15. Which sentence tells an opinion? Tell if you agree or disagree.

A. Buses are the best way to travel in a city.

B. People in cities can travel on subways and buses.

Unit 3 Activities

 Unit Writing Activity

Write a Descriptive Paragraph Think about the place where you live.

■ Write a paragraph that describes your community.

■ Give facts and details.

 Unit Project

Community Calendar Make a calendar of special events in your community.

■ Use reference materials to find out about special events.

■ Show the events on a calendar. Draw pictures of them.

Read More

■ **Country Kid, City Kid** by Julie Cummins. Henry Holt and Company, 2002.

■ **Food from Farms** by Nancy Dickmann. Heinemann Educational Books, 2010.

■ **Living in Suburban Communities** by Kristin Sterling. Lerner Classroom, 2007.

Go Digital **Education Place®** visit www.eduplace.com/nycssp/

Unit 4

Rights, Rules, and Responsibilities

The Big Idea

What is the relationship between local government and the community?

WHAT TO KNOW

✓ Why are rules and laws important?

✓ How do we honor our country?

✓ How are state and national leaders elected?

✓ Who are the people who take part in New York City government?

✓ What public services does New York City's government provide?

Public Services in New York City

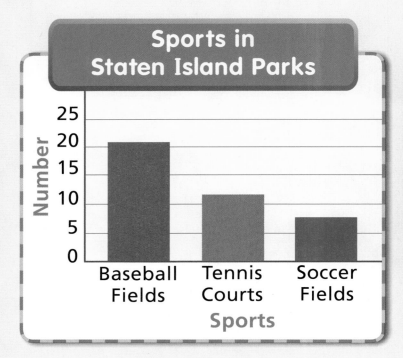

Sports in Staten Island Parks

A postal worker delivers mail

NEW JERSEY

Playground at Brooklyn Bridge Park

Upper
New
York
Bay

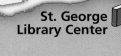
St. George
Library Center

Fort
Wadsworth

**Staten
Island**

Miller
Field

Great
Kills
Park

NEW YORK

Long Island Sound

NEW JERSEY

Van Cortlandt Park

Bronx Library Center

Bronx Park

Pelham Bay Park

Bronx

Hudson River

East River

Manhattan

Central Park

New York Public Library

Queens Library

Flushing Meadows-Corona Park

Queens

Forest Park

Brooklyn Public Library

Prospect Park

Brooklyn

Jamaica Bay

Lower New York Bay

North
West · East
South

ATLANTIC OCEAN

Map Key	
🏛 City hall	▨ Park
⛑ Fire station	🛡 Police station
✚ Hospital	✉ Post office
📖 Library	

Reading Social Studies

Categorize

Why It Matters You can categorize information to help you understand what you read.

Learn the Skill

■ When you categorize, you decide if something fits in a group.

■ Decide what each group will be called. Place each thing into a group.

Read the paragraph below.

Categorize

The state of New York has many symbols. These symbols stand for the state. Some symbols are plants. The rose is the state flower of New York. The sugar maple is the state tree. Some symbols are animals. The bluebird is the state bird. The ladybug is the state insect. Food symbols include the apple and the apple muffin. Symbols can be objects, too. The state flag and state seal are both symbols.

Practice the Skill

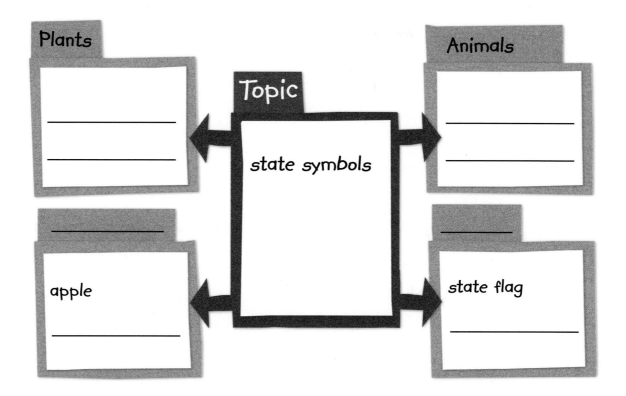

Plants

Topic

state symbols

Animals

apple

state flag

Copy this chart to categorize things that are symbols of New York. Two of the groups, <u>Plants</u> and <u>Animals,</u> are already named. Name the other two groups. List the symbols that go in each group.

Apply the Skill

As you read this unit, look for ways to categorize information about New York City.

Vocabulary Preview

law

A **law** is a rule that citizens must follow. One law says drivers must stop at stop signs. **page 159**

landmark

The Washington Monument is a famous landmark. A **landmark** is a feature that makes a place special. **page 168**

election

An **election** is a time when people vote. You can hold a class election to make a choice. page 175

public service

A **public service** is a service that government provides for citizens.

page 192

Go Digital   visit www.eduplace.com/nycssp/

Communities Have Rules and Laws

What to Know
Why are rules and laws important?

Vocabulary
rule
law
consequence
judge

Reading Skill
Categorize

Before You Read

What are some rules in your classroom or school?

Rules Are Important

Most groups have rules. A **rule** helps people know what they should and should not do. Rules help people get along. In some groups, people talk about rules. They may make or change their rules together.

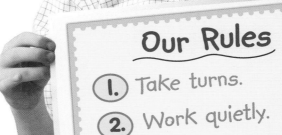

Our Rules
1. Take turns.
2. Work quietly.
3. Be kind to others.

A **law** is a rule that everyone in a community, state, or country must follow. Rules and laws protect our rights and help us stay safe. They help us learn, work, and play together. Rules and laws also help us solve problems fairly.

main idea

✓ **Reading Check** **Categorize** If a group decides that there can be no running in the classroom, is that a rule or a law?

Communities have traffic laws to keep people safe on the roads.

Making and Following Laws

Citizens choose leaders to make laws. Leaders meet to talk about problems and make laws to solve them. Police tell people how to obey laws. They stop people who break laws. Look at the picture on the next page. What might be happening? Think of another way police help with laws.

Street signs show laws everyone must follow.

The consequence of breaking a parking law is getting a ticket.

People who break laws must face consequences. A **consequence** is something that happens because of what a person does. A **judge** helps decide if someone has broken a law and what the consequence will be. A person who breaks a traffic law often has to pay money to the city. When people don't agree about laws, a judge decides what the law means.

Parking Violation

☐ Letting the meter run out

☑ Blocking a fire hydrant

☐ Double-parking

Fine.........$65

✓ Reading Check Draw Conclusions What do you think would happen if there were no traffic laws?

Rules and Laws in the Community

Rules and laws help people share places and things in the community. There are laws about keeping parks clean. Parks are places that belong to everyone. When you follow laws in a park, you help others enjoy the park. There are rules about taking books from public libraries. Books must be returned on time so others can use them.

Water is a resource people in the community must share. Laws tell how and when people can use fire hydrants to cool off on hot summer days.

Communities change over time. Rules and laws change, too. In the past, people could walk their dogs without leashes. Now many states have leash laws. People must keep their dogs on a leash when they are in public places. Some communities have a rule that people must clean up after their dogs.

✓ **Reading Check** **Problem and Solution** How do people solve the problem of sharing places in the community?

Lesson Review

❶ **What to Know** Why are rules and laws important?

❷ **Vocabulary** Use the words **judge** and **consequence** in a sentence.

❸ **Categorize** Who stops people who break laws?

❹ **Art Activity** Draw a picture of a street sign you have seen. Explain the law it tells people to follow.

Resolve a Conflict

▶ **Vocabulary**

conflict

People in classrooms and communities don't always agree. When people disagree, it is called a **conflict**. Together, people can resolve conflicts.

Learn the Skill

Follow the steps to help resolve a conflict.

Step 1 Imagine you and your friend want to use the computer at the same time.

Step 2 Think about what each person wants to do on the computer.

Write	Play Games

Step 3 Think of ways to resolve the conflict.
- Take turns.
- Write using a pencil and paper.
- Play a board game.

Step 4 Ask yourself about each idea: Can both people do some of what they want? Choose the best way to resolve the conflict.

Work with a small group. Look at the picture below. Then follow the directions.

1 Tell in your own words what the conflict is. What does each group want?

2 List some ways to resolve the conflict.

Choose the solution you think is best. Write a paragraph telling why you think the solution will work.

Symbols of Our Country

What to Know
How do we honor our country?

Vocabulary
symbol
landmark
monument

Reading Skill
Main Idea and Details

Before You Read

Every morning at school you stand and place your hand over your heart. What are you doing?

Important Symbols

Citizens of the United States come from different backgrounds. Yet they salute the same flag. The United States flag is a symbol for all Americans. A **symbol** is a picture, place, or thing that stands for another thing or idea.

The bald eagle is a symbol of freedom.

People in all parts of the United States remember to honor their country when they see American symbols. The American flag is the symbol people most often use for the United States. There are rules about how to treat the flag with respect.

The bald eagle is another symbol of the United States. So is Uncle Sam. You can see symbols of the United States on coins and stamps.

A pledge is a kind of promise. When we say the Pledge of Allegiance, we promise to respect the flag and our country.

✓ **Reading Check** **Main Idea and Details** Why are American symbols important?

Landmarks and Monuments

A **landmark** is a feature that makes a location special. A sign or statue may be a landmark. <u>Many landmarks are symbols for the United States.</u>

Statue of Liberty, New York City

This statue is 151 feet tall. France gave the statue to the United States as a gift. It was a sign of friendship. For many years, the statue welcomed immigrants to America. Today, people can visit this symbol of freedom.

Washington Monument, Washington, D.C.

A **monument** is a building or statue that honors a hero or an event. The Washington Monument honors George Washington. He was the first President of the United States. He was known for being brave, strong, and honest.

Mount Rushmore, South Dakota

An artist and many helpers carved the faces of four important Presidents into the stone of a mountain. It took them 14 years to finish the project. Each President's head is as tall as a six-story building. Their noses are 20 feet long!

✓ **Reading Check** **Compare and Contrast** How are the Washington Monument and Mount Rushmore alike?

George Washington

Thomas Jefferson

Theodore Roosevelt

Abraham Lincoln

Honoring America

The United States has many holidays, or days on which we celebrate or remember something. Some holidays honor our country's heroes. Other holidays help us remember important events.

Dr. Martin Luther King, Jr. Day in January honors a hero who worked for fair laws. In February, we celebrate Presidents' Day. Both George Washington and Abraham Lincoln were born in February. We honor these Presidents for leading our country.

✓ **Reading Check** **Sequence** Which holiday comes first during the year, Dr. Martin Luther King, Jr. Day or Presidents' Day?

We celebrate Memorial Day at the end of May. On this day we honor the men and women who gave their lives for our country.

Independence Day is also called the Fourth of July.
It is the birthday of the United States. On this day
in 1776, America declared its independence.

Lesson Review

1. **What to Know** How do we honor our country?

2. **Vocabulary** Write a sentence about the Statue of Liberty that uses the word **landmark**.

3. **Main Idea and Details** Name three symbols of the United States.

4. **Art Activity** Choose someone you would like to honor with a special holiday. Draw a picture to show how it would be celebrated. Add a caption to your picture.

The Star-Spangled Banner

Today, you can see the flag Key wrote about at a Smithsonian museum.

The year was 1814. The United States was at war. All night Francis Scott Key watched British cannons fire on an American fort. Key could see the American flag flying over the fort. That proved that the enemy had not won the battle.

Key was so proud, he wrote a poem. Someone added a tune to the poem, and Americans started to sing the words Key had written. The song became the national anthem of the United States. An anthem is a song that is a symbol of a place.

Oh, say can you see, by the dawn's early light,

What so proudly we hailed at the twilight's last gleaming?

Whose broad stripes and bright stars,
  through the perilous fight,

O'er the ramparts we watched,
  were so gallantly streaming?

And the rockets' red glare, the bombs bursting in air,

Gave proof through the night that our flag was still there.

O say, does that star-spangled banner yet wave

O'er the land of the free and the home of the brave?

Activities

1. **Talk About It** Explain why a national anthem is important to a country.

2. **Draw It** Draw a picture of a person or people singing the national anthem. Under the picture, write a few words about how they feel.

 Go Digital Visit Education Place for more primary sources. www. eduplace.com/nycssp/

Lesson 3

What to Know

How are state and national leaders elected?

Vocabulary

government
election
governor
vote

Reading Skill

Draw Conclusions

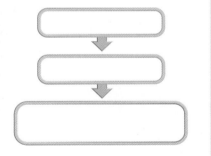

State and National Leaders

New York City is part of New York State. Both the city and the state have their own governments. A **government** is a group of citizens that runs a community, state, or country.

main idea

Lawmakers meet at the capitol building in Albany to make decisions.

State Government

Citizens choose many government leaders in events called **elections**. People choose the leaders they think will do the best job.

People in New York choose a **governor** to lead the state. They also choose people to make laws for New York State. Only citizens of New York State can choose state leaders.

✓ **Reading Check** **Draw Conclusions** What is the purpose of elections?

National Government

Citizens from every state vote to choose leaders for the whole country. When people **vote,** they make a choice that gets counted.

Our country's government is divided into three parts, or branches. Each branch has a building in the nation's capital, Washington, D.C. Leaders meet there to make decisions for the country.

✓ **Reading Check** **Main Idea and Details** How many branches does the national government have?

The White House

The President of the United States is the leader of the nation. People vote for a President every four years. The President lives and works in the White House.

Capitol

Supreme Court

Members of Congress make laws. People from each state vote for their senators and representatives. Congress works in the Capitol Building.

The Supreme Court has nine judges. They are chosen by the President. Congress has to agree on each choice. The judges decide if laws are fair and protect citizens' rights. They meet in the Supreme Court Building.

Governments Solve Problems

City, state, and national governments make laws to solve different kinds of problems. New York City government only makes laws for the city. A city law might say where you can park a car. The New York State government makes laws for people in the whole state. States make laws about how old you must be to drive a car. People in New York City and New York State must also follow national laws. One national law says you must be 18 years old to vote.

main idea

✔ **Reading Check** **Cause and Effect** Which type of government affects the most people?

Government leaders must work together to solve problems.

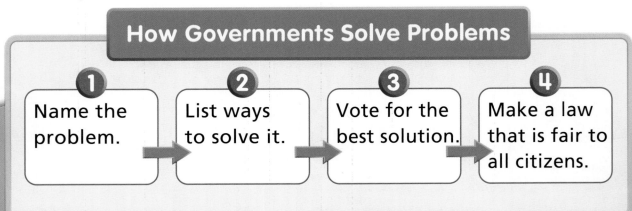

How Governments Solve Problems

1 Name the problem. → **2** List ways to solve it. → **3** Vote for the best solution. → **4** Make a law that is fair to all citizens.

Skill **Reading Charts** What do government leaders do after they list ways to solve a problem?

❶ What to Know

How are state and national leaders elected?

❷ Draw Conclusions

Why do we need local, state, and national governments?

❸ Case Study Detective

Look at the two pictures. Someone wearing this sticker has been in a booth like this one. Choose the name of the booth:

- toll booth
- voting booth
- ticket booth

❹ Word Play

Part of the word <u>President</u> is "preside," which means "to be in charge of something." Use the letters in <u>President</u> to spell other words. Here are three words.

pride   rest   tie

New Yorkers *in* Government

Many New Yorkers have been leaders in local, state, and national government.

Franklin and Eleanor Roosevelt were both national leaders. Franklin was elected governor of New York State in 1924. He became President of the United States in 1933. As First Lady, Eleanor traveled to many places to learn about the problems of Americans. She worked with the Red Cross and the United Nations to help people in the United States and around the world.

Nelson Rockefeller was governor of New York State from 1958 to 1973. He loved great art. He started some of the world's greatest art museums in New York City. Rockefeller made transportation and education in New York better. He also helped start 55 new state parks. In 1974, he became Vice-President of the United States.

David Dinkins was elected borough president of Manhattan in 1985. He became the first African American mayor of New York City on January 1, 1990.

Kirsten Gillibrand was born in rural New York State. In 2009, she became a United States senator. As a senator, she works for the whole state of New York in the national government.

Sonia Sotomayor grew up in the South Bronx. Her parents came to New York City from Puerto Rico. Sonia became a lawyer and a judge. In 2009, she became the first Puerto Rican member of the United States Supreme Court.

Activities

1. **Talk About It** How have these New Yorkers helped their state or country?

2. **Present It** Find out about another government leader from New York. Present two facts about the leader to your class.

🔍 **CASE STUDY**

New York City Government

▶ What to Know

Who are the people who take part in New York City government?

▶ Vocabulary

mayor
city council

🎯 Reading Skill

Main Idea and Details

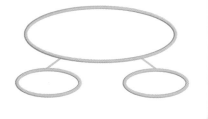

New York City's government is the largest city government in the United States. <u>Many people are needed to make decisions and plans for the largest city in our country.</u> *(main idea* ⭐ *)*

City Leaders

The **mayor** is the leader of the city. The **city council** is a group of people chosen to make laws. The mayor and city council work together to decide how to use money for schools, police, parks, and other community needs.

New York City has its own flag.

City leaders visit schools in their community.

Each New York City borough has a president. Borough presidents lead their boroughs. They help the mayor make decisions about each borough.

New York City also has 59 community boards. Each board has 50 members. The community boards help make decisions and solve problems in their local communities.

✓ Reading Check **Main Idea and Details** Who leads New York City boroughs?

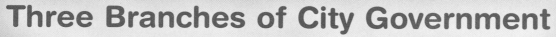

Three Branches of City Government

Just like the national government, the government of New York City has three branches. People in each branch have different roles and responsibilities.

✓ **Reading Check** **Categorize** What do deputy mayors do?

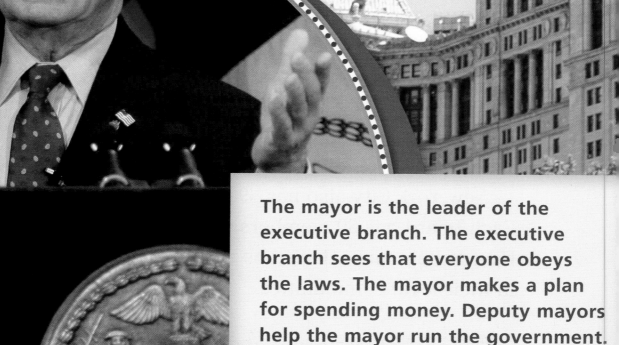

The mayor is the leader of the executive branch. The executive branch sees that everyone obeys the laws. The mayor makes a plan for spending money. Deputy mayors help the mayor run the government.

The city council is the legislative branch. It makes laws. The city council has 51 members.

The judicial branch of the government includes judges and courts. Judges decide what to do when people break laws.

Leaders and Citizens

Citizens can take part in New York City's government. They can go to meetings to talk about problems and share ideas. They can vote for the mayor and city council members. Some citizens may decide they want to work in government. If enough people vote for them, they can become leaders, too!

main idea

✓ **Reading Check** **Main Idea and Details** What are some ways citizens can take part in city government?

Building fences will make our playgrounds safer.

Will you add more bus stops?

CASE STUDY REVIEW

❶ What to Know

Who are the people who take part in
New York City government?

❷ Main Idea and Details

Why are so many people needed to run
New York City's government?

❸ Case Study Detective

Which statement would someone
wearing this button likely make?
- ★ Call me if you need help in the pool.
- ★ Vote for me, and I will make
  city streets cleaner.
- ★ My bank will take care of your money.

VOTE
for your
MAYOR

❹ Word Play

Read the list below. Write the circled letters on the
blanks to find the answer to the riddle.

Citizens can:
go to meetings
vote for leaders
run for office
tell the mayor what they think about problems
What makes New York City run?

_____ _____ _____ _____ _____ _____ _____ _____ _____

The United Nations

The United Nations, or UN, was started by a group of countries in 1945. The United States was one of 51 countries that joined the UN during the first year. The goal of the UN is to help countries work together to build peace.

Today, more than 190 nations belong to the United Nations. People from these nations meet at the UN headquarters in New York City.

Japan

Jordan

Liberia

Luxembourg

People from UN member nations meet in this room to discuss problems and find solutions.

Mexico

Activities

1. **Talk About It** Why do you think countries might join the United Nations?

2. **Write About It** Visitors can take tours of the UN headquarters. What are two questions you would ask if you took a tour of the UN building?

Lesson 5

City Government At work

What to Know

What public services does New York City's government provide?

Vocabulary

public service

department

tax

Reading Skill

Main Idea and Details

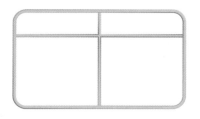

Governments provide many public services for people. A **public service** is a service that is available to everyone. Local, state, and national governments each help with different services.

The post office is a public service. The national government runs the post office. State roads are another public service. They are taken care of by the states.

Post offices take people's letters and packages where they need to go.

New York City Hall

City Services

People who work for the government of New York City help provide public services. Many of them work in City Hall. City Hall is a symbol of New York City government.

Other government workers work in different parts of the city. They teach in schools. They make sure people have clean water. They protect citizens and fight fires. They run libraries. Some judges are also city workers. They work in government buildings called courthouses.

✓ **Reading Check** **Main Idea and Details** What is one public service New York City government provides?

City Departments

More than 300,000 people work for the government of New York City. They work in different departments. Each **department** has a special job in the government.

✓ **Reading Check** **Categorize** Which city department would you call if you wanted a booklet about healthy eating?

Department:	Department of Education
What It Does:	runs schools
Who Works in It:	teachers, principals, maintenance workers, cafeteria staff
Where They Work:	schools

Department:	Department of Health
What It Does:	helps people stay healthy
Who Works in It:	doctors, nurses, social workers, food inspectors
Where They Work:	hospitals, clinics, restaurants

Burn Calories, Not Electricity

Take the Stairs!
Walking up the stairs just 2 minutes a day helps prevent weight gain. It also helps the environment.

Department:	Department of Transportation
What It Does:	runs buses and subways, repairs roads and bridges
Who Works in It:	drivers, construction workers, traffic planners
Where They Work:	streets, tunnels, bridges

Department:	Department of Sanitation
What It Does:	recycles, removes trash, cleans streets
Who Works in It:	sanitation workers, truck drivers
Where They Work:	streets, sidewalks, recycling center

Paying for Public Services

How do governments pay for public services? City, state, and national governments collect money called **taxes**. Workers pay income taxes from the money they earn. Businesses also pay taxes. In most states, people pay sales taxes when they buy goods such as bikes or baseball gloves. Governments use money from taxes to pay workers, buy what they need, and care for the buildings used to provide public services.

✓ **Reading Check** **Problem and Solution** How do governments pay for public services?

Taxes help pay for community resources such as playgrounds.

CASE STUDY REVIEW

❶ What to Know

What public services does New York City's government provide?

❷ Main Idea and Details

Why are government services important?

❸ Case Study Detective

When you buy something in New York City, the total amount you pay includes a tax. How much tax was paid on this baseball glove and ball? How can you tell?

Baseball	$7.00
Baseball glove	$35.00
SUBTOTAL	$42.00
New York City Tax 9%	$3.78
TOTAL	$45.78
Cash Paid	$50.00
Change	$4.22

❹ Word Play

Fill in the blanks to name the correct department.

A worker in the Department of

__ __ __ __ a t i o n could teach second graders.

A worker in the Department of

__ __ __ __ __ a t i o n could take glass bottles to a recycling center.

A worker in the Department of

__ __ __ __ __ __ __ __ __ a t i o n could drive a city bus.

Skillbuilder

Make a Decision

Good citizens think before they make decisions. To make a **decision**, you make up your mind. It may help to compare choices in a chart.

► **Vocabulary**

decision

Learn the Skill

Suppose that your class wants to do a project that helps the school. The children in your class like two different ideas. How do you make a decision?

Step 1 Put the ideas in a chart that shows what is good about each choice. Use plus (+) for good and minus (–) for bad. Look at the example on this page.

Step 2 Think and talk about what is good and bad about each choice. Write your thoughts in the chart.

Step 3 Compare choices in the chart. You might ask: Which choice will help more people in the school? Decide which choice is better.

School Clean-up Day	School Garden
+ School will look better More school pride	+ Beautiful flowers Healthful vegetables
– Hard work Not fun	– Takes too long Might not grow well

Look at the pictures and read the words. Tell what Gabriel's choices are. Follow the directions.

1 Make a chart to show what is good and bad about each choice.

2 Think of a question Gabriel might ask to help him decide.

Want to play soccer after you finish raking?

Want to go to a movie after we finish raking?

I can't decide!

Apply the Skill

Use the question and the chart to help Gabriel make a decision. Write a paragraph explaining why it was the best decision.

Fun Town Walk

SCHOOL

Park Ranger

Police Station

Police Officer

CITY PARK

Teacher

Match the workers who provide public services to the places where they work. Then, name three other government workers you learned about. Tell where they might work.

Fire Station

LIBRARY

CITY HALL

Principal

Mayor

MAYOR

Firefighter

Librarian

Go Digital **Education Place**®
www.eduplace.com

Visit Eduplace!

Log on to Eduplace to explore Social Studies online. Play now at **www.eduplace.com/nycssp/**

Reading Social Studies

When you **categorize**, you sort things into groups.

 Categorize

1. Complete the graphic organizer to show that you understand how to sort things into groups.

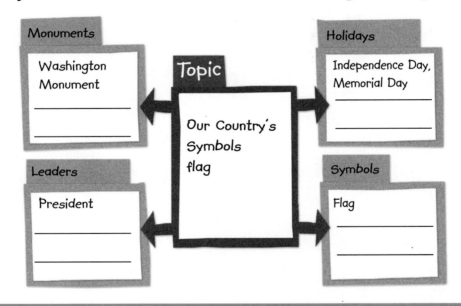

Monuments

Washington Monument

_____

_____

Topic

Our Country's Symbols
flag

Holidays

Independence Day, Memorial Day

_____

_____

Leaders

President

_____

_____

Symbols

Flag

_____

_____

 Write About the Big Idea

2. **Write Questions** Local government is part of a community. Write three questions you would like to ask a local government leader in an interview.

Vocabulary

Match the word to its meaning.

3. a feature that makes a location special

4. a service available to everyone

5. a rule that everyone must follow

6. a time when people vote

7. a group of people who work together to run a city, state, or country

A. **law** (page 159)

B. **landmark** (page 168)

C. **government** (page 174)

D. **election** (page 175)

E. **public service** (page 192)

Facts and Main Ideas

Write a sentence to answer each question.

8. Why do we celebrate national holidays?

9. How do people choose government leaders?

10. What group makes laws in New York City?

Critical Thinking

Write a short answer for each question.

11. **Draw Conclusions** Why have laws changed over time?

12. **Analyze** What helps to unite Americans who come from different backgrounds?

13. Look at the picture. What conflict does the picture show?

14. Choose the best way to resolve the conflict.

A

B

C

Make a Decision

15. What can Nora do? Name two or three choices.

16. Make a chart for each choice to show what is good or bad about it.

Good	Bad

17. What should Nora choose? Tell reasons for your decision.

Unit 4 Activities

 ## Unit Writing Activity

Write a Speech What idea do you have that would help the citizens of your community?

- Write a speech about a problem in your community.
- Tell how you think it can be solved.

 ## Unit Project

Role-Play Role-play how a city council makes laws.

- Practice presenting opinions.
- Role-play a council meeting and write a new law.

Read More

- **What's a Mayor?** by Nancy Harris. Heinemann Educational Books, 2007.
- **What Presidents Are Made Of** by Hanoch Piven. Atheneum, 2004.
- **D Is for Democracy: A Citizen's Alphabet** by Elissa Grodin. Sleeping Bear Press, 2007.

Go Digital **Education Place®** visit www.eduplace.com/nycssp/

Resources

The Five Themes of Geography

Learning about places is an important part of history and geography. When geographers talk about Earth, they think about five themes, or main ideas.

GEOGRAPHY

Location

Everything on Earth has its own place.

Place

Every place has features that make it different from other places.

Human-Environment Interactions

People can change their surroundings.

Movement

Each day, people around the world trade goods and ideas.

THEMES

Regions

Areas of Earth share features that make them different from other areas.

Atlas

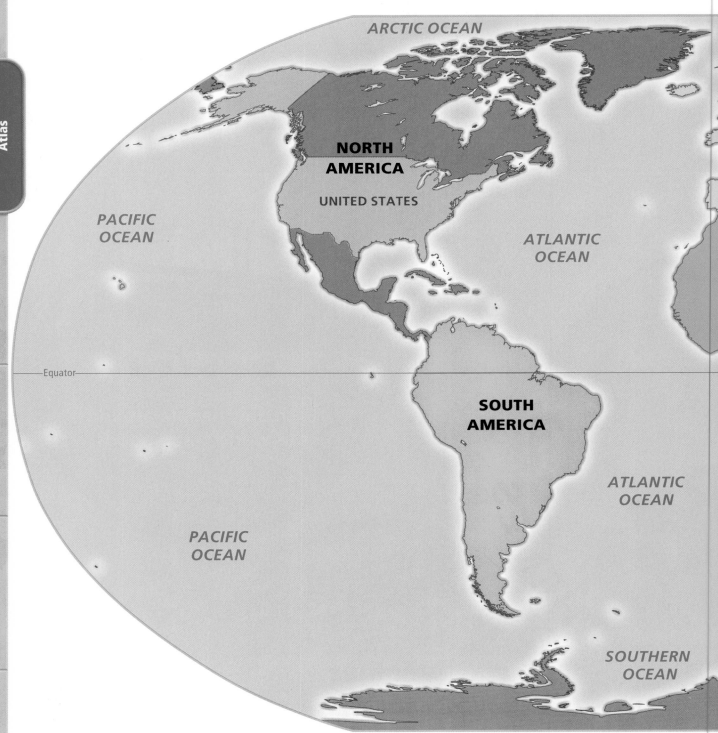

ARCTIC OCEAN

PACIFIC
OCEAN

NORTH
AMERICA

UNITED STATES

ATLANTIC
OCEAN

Equator

SOUTH
AMERICA

ATLANTIC
OCEAN

PACIFIC
OCEAN

SOUTHERN
OCEAN

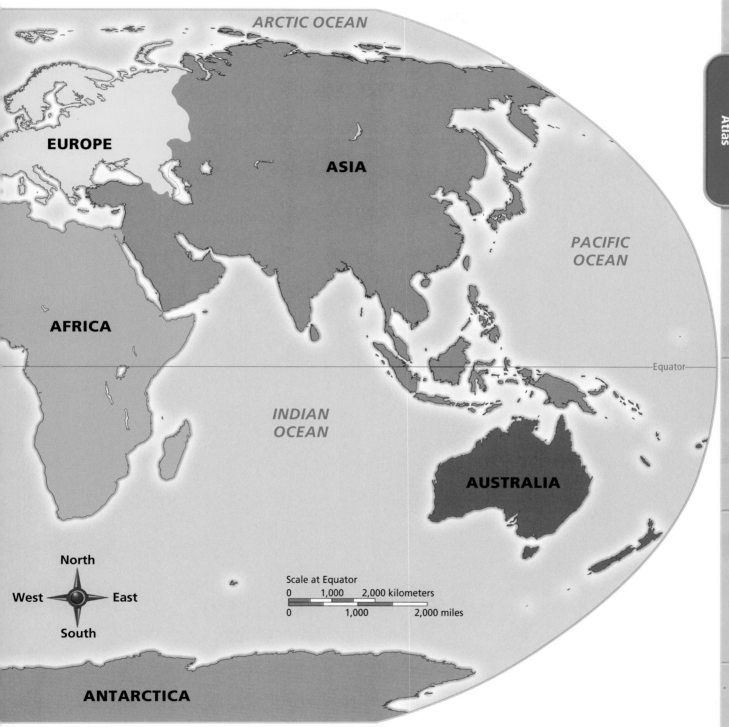

ARCTIC OCEAN

EUROPE

ASIA

PACIFIC
OCEAN

AFRICA

Equator

INDIAN
OCEAN

AUSTRALIA

North

West — East

South

ANTARCTICA

Scale at Equator

0   1,000   2,000 kilometers

0   1,000   2,000 miles

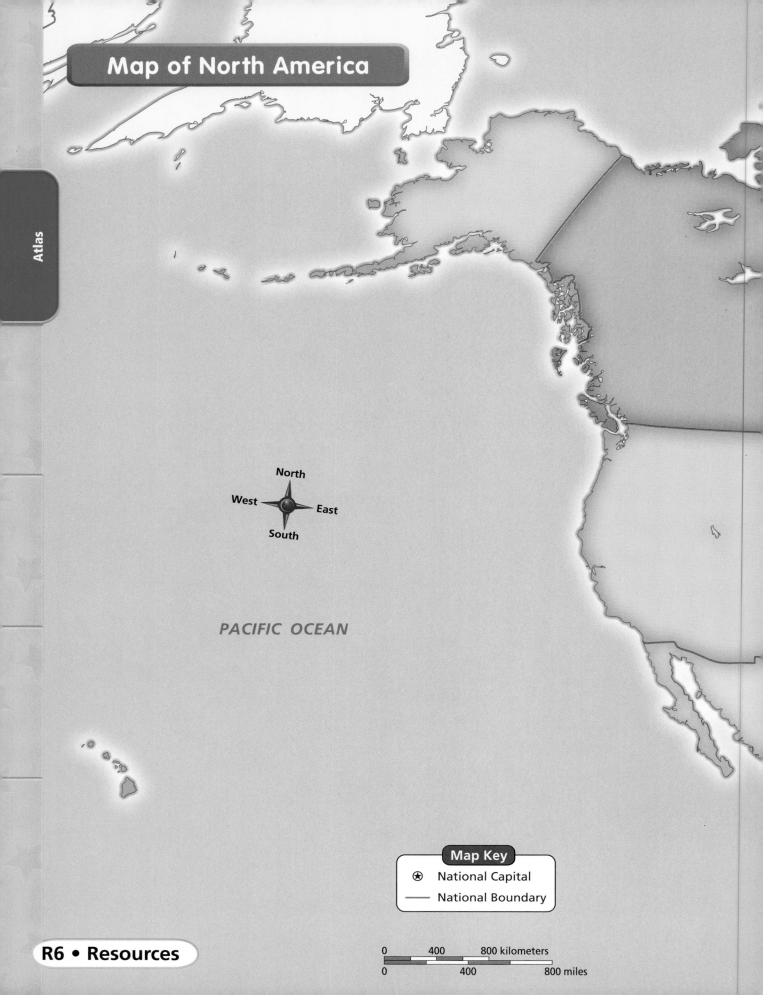

Map of North America

North

West —✦— East

South

PACIFIC OCEAN

Map Key

⊛ National Capital

— National Boundary

0	400	800 kilometers
0	400	800 miles

CANADA

UNITED STATES

MEXICO

Ottawa

Washington, D.C.

ATLANTIC
OCEAN

Mexico City

Map of the United States

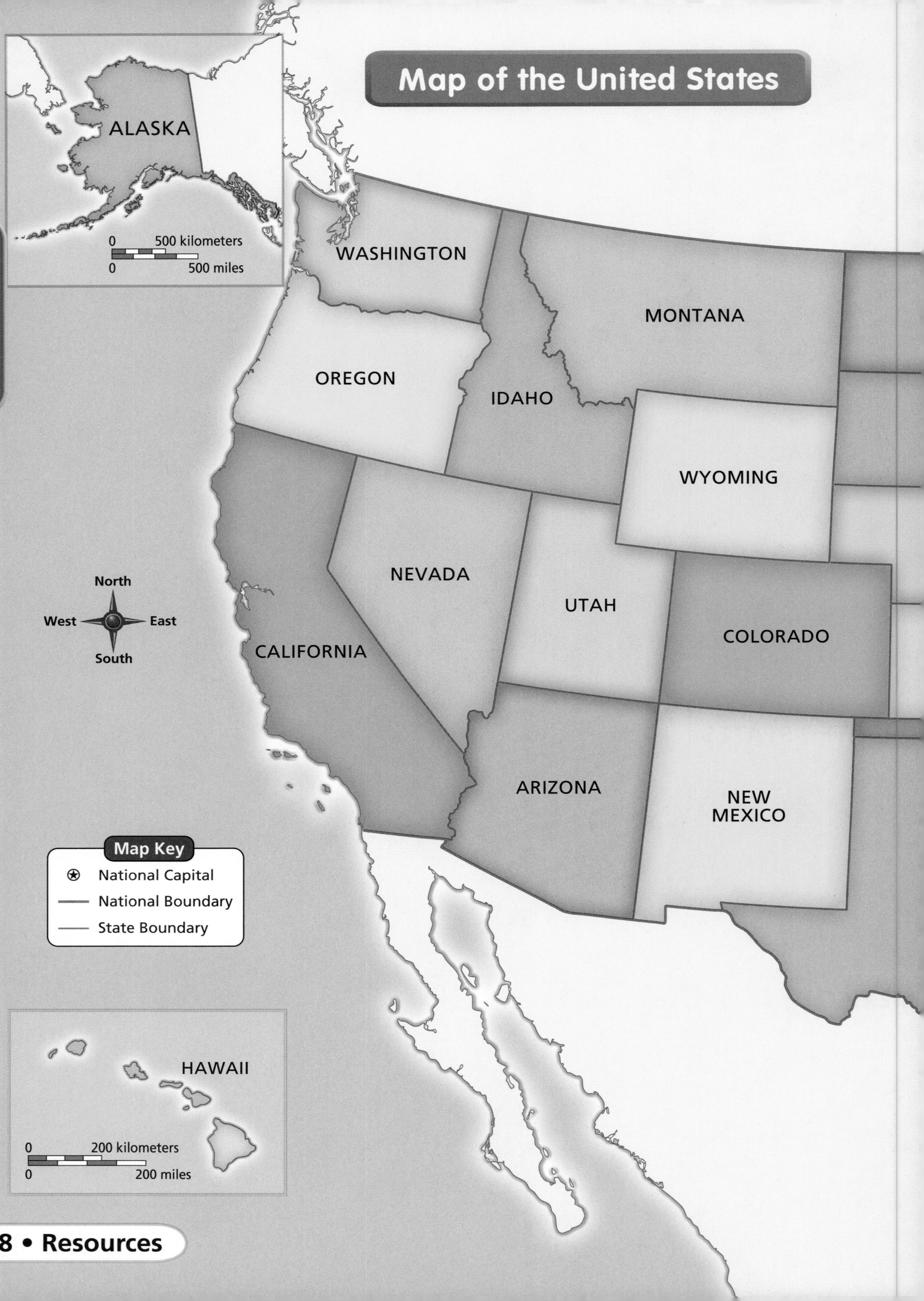

ALASKA

0   500 kilometers
0   500 miles

WASHINGTON

OREGON

MONTANA

IDAHO

WYOMING

North
West — East
South

NEVADA

UTAH

COLORADO

CALIFORNIA

ARIZONA

NEW
MEXICO

Map Key

⊛ National Capital

— National Boundary

— State Boundary

HAWAII

0   200 kilometers
0   200 miles

NORTH DAKOTA

MINNESOTA

SOUTH DAKOTA

WISCONSIN

MICHIGAN

NEW HAMPSHIRE

VERMONT

MAINE

MASSACHUSETTS

NEW YORK

RHODE ISLAND

CONNECTICUT

NEW JERSEY

DELAWARE

Washington, D.C.

MARYLAND

PENNSYLVANIA

NEBRASKA

IOWA

ILLINOIS

INDIANA

OHIO

WEST VIRGINIA

VIRGINIA

KANSAS

MISSOURI

KENTUCKY

NORTH CAROLINA

TENNESSEE

SOUTH CAROLINA

OKLAHOMA

ARKANSAS

ALABAMA

GEORGIA

MISSISSIPPI

TEXAS

LOUISIANA

FLORIDA

0   125   250 kilometers
0   125   250 miles

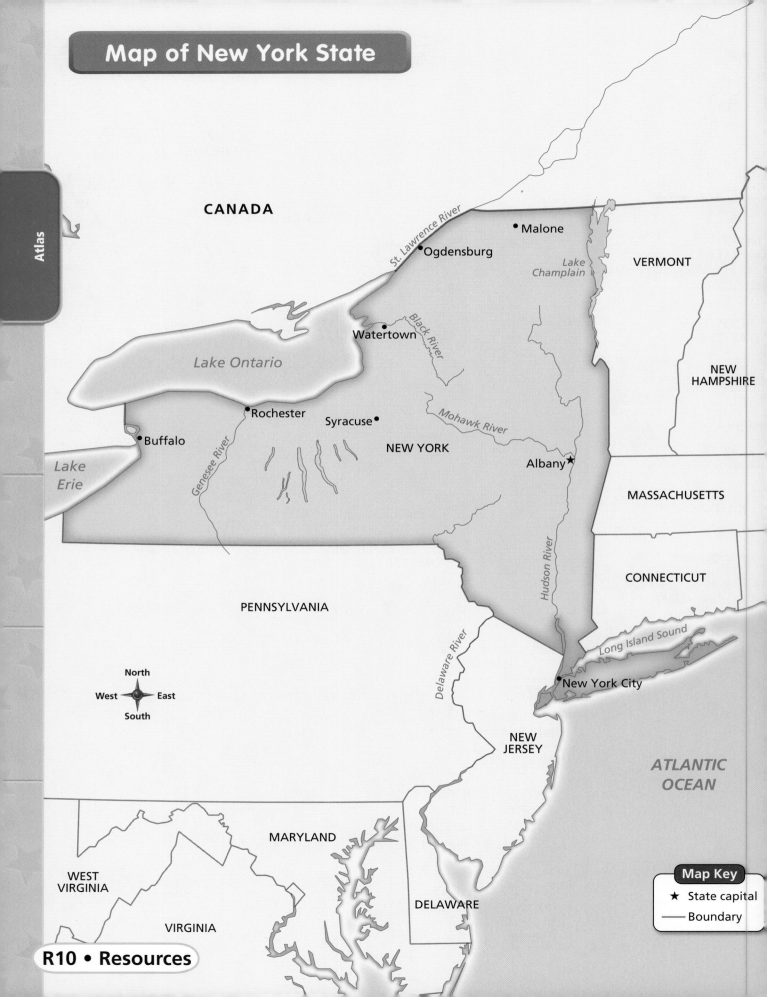

Map of New York State

CANADA

Malone

St. Lawrence River

Ogdensburg

Lake Champlain

VERMONT

Watertown

Black River

Lake Ontario

NEW HAMPSHIRE

Rochester

Syracuse

Mohawk River

NEW YORK

Genesee River

Buffalo

Lake Erie

Albany

MASSACHUSETTS

Hudson River

CONNECTICUT

PENNSYLVANIA

Delaware River

Long Island Sound

North

West · East

South

New York City

NEW JERSEY

ATLANTIC OCEAN

WEST VIRGINIA

MARYLAND

VIRGINIA

DELAWARE

Map Key

★ State capital

— Boundary

Map of New York City Boroughs

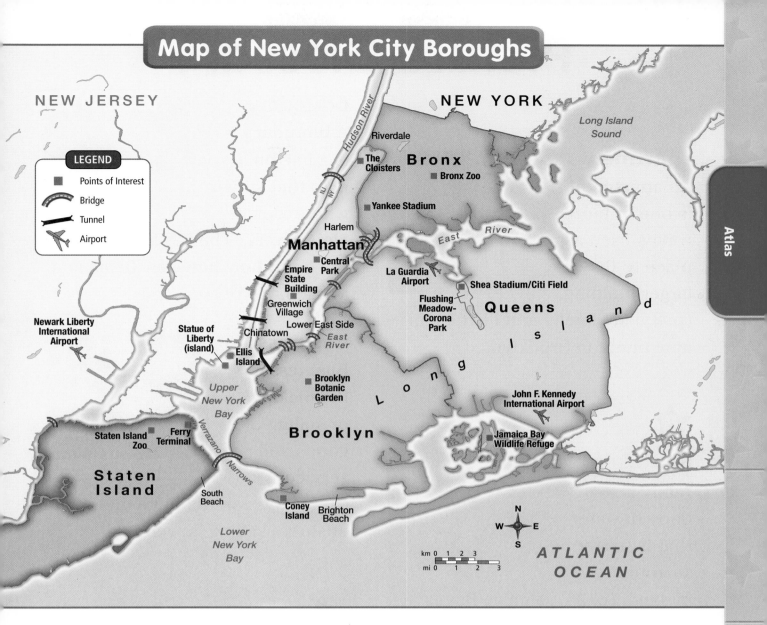

Borough	Origin of Name
The Bronx	For Mr. and Mrs. Bronck (the Broncks), a Danish man and his Dutch wife, the first settlers there to buy land from Native Americans
Brooklyn	For a town in the Netherlands
Manhattan	From the Lenape word for "island"
Queens	For Queen Catherine, who was Queen of England when the English took control of New Netherland in 1664
Staten Island	From the Dutch word for "state" or " government"; the Dutch government took over the island in 1637

Picture Glossary

apartment

An **apartment** is one or more rooms used as a place to live in a larger building.
(p. 85) My family and I live in an **apartment** in Brooklyn.

bay

A **bay** is a body of water that is partly surrounded by land. (p. 26) Jamaica Bay is located in New York City.

borough

A **borough** is a part of a city. (p. 19) Queens is one of the five **boroughs** of New York City.

boundary

A **boundary** is a line on a map that shows where a place ends. (p. 11) The red line shows the **boundary** between Texas and Mexico.

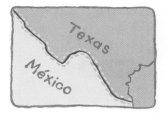

business

Business is the making or selling of goods and services.
(p. 71) My parents have their own **business** selling flowers.

canal

A **canal** is a river made by people. (p. 28) In the past, **canals** were used to ship goods.

Picture Glossary

cardinal directions

Cardinal directions are the main directions of north, south, east, and west. (p. 16) **Cardinal directions** help you find places on a map.

North
West   East
South

change

A **change** is what happens when something becomes different. (p. 62) Tall buildings **changed** the way New York City looks.

citizen

A **citizen** is a person who belongs to a place. (p. 18) You are a **citizen** of the community where you live.

city council

A **city council** is a group of people chosen to make laws and solve problems. (p. 184) The **city council** meets at City Hall.

climate

The kind of weather a place has over a long time is called **climate**. (p. 116) New York has a **climate** with cold winters and warm summers.

colony

A **colony** is a land that is ruled by another country. (p. 69) New York was an English **colony** named after the Duke of York.

communication

Communication is the sharing of ideas and information. (p. 74) The telephone is an important form of **communication**.

community

A **community** is a place where groups of people live. (p. 10) Cities and towns are **communities**.

commute

To **commute** is to travel between home and work. (p. 130) People use cars, trains, and buses to **commute**.

compass rose

The symbol on a map that shows directions is called a **compass rose.** (p. 16) Use the **compass rose** to find north.

North
West East
South

conflict

A **conflict** is a disagreement. (p. 164) Good citizens try to resolve **conflicts** peacefully.

consequence

A **consequence** is something that happens because of what a person does. (p. 161) The **consequence** of breaking a parking law is getting a ticket.

PARKING VIOLATION
☐ Letting the meter run out
☑ Blocking a fire hydrant
☐ Double-parking
Fine.............$65

continent

A **continent** is a large area of land. (p. 14) Earth has seven **continents.**

country

A **country** is a land where people have the same laws and leaders. (p. 20) Mexico is a **country** south of the United States.

UNITED STATES
MEXICO

culture

The way of life of a group of people is called a **culture.** (p. 86) Clothing, language, and food are all part of a person's **culture.**

D

decision

A **decision** is a choice. (p. 198) I had to make a **decision** to do my homework before or after dinner.

department

A **department** is a part of an organized system. (p. 194) The city government has many **departments.**

dictionary

A **dictionary** is a book that gives the meanings of words. (p. 118) Look up new words in a **dictionary.**

E

election

An **election** is a time when people vote for their leaders. (p. 175) We have an **election** to choose our President every four years.

elevator

An **elevator** is a moving platform that moves people and things between floors in a tall building. (p. 80) Skyscrapers need **elevators.**

encyclopedia

An **encyclopedia** is a book or set of books that gives information about many topics. (p. 118) Look up a topic in an **encyclopedia** to learn more about it.

environment

The **environment** is all of the things that people find around them. (p. 44) Land, water, plants, animals, and people are all part of the **environment.**

equator

An **equator** is an imaginary line that divides Earth into northern and southern halves. (p. 22) You can only see the **equator** on maps.

explorer

An **explorer** is a person who travels to find new things and places. (p. 66) Christopher Columbus was an **explorer** who traveled to the Americas.

fact

A **fact** is something that is true. (p. 126) A book about seashells has many **facts** in it.

factory

A **factory** is a building where people use machines to make goods. (p. 92) Many people work at the **factory.**

farming

Farming means growing crops or raising animals. (p. 138) Rural areas have enough space for **farming**.

geography

Geography is the study of Earth and its people. (p. 34) **Geography** teaches us about Earth and the people on it.

globe

A **globe** is a model of Earth. (p. 14) We can find the United States on a **globe.**

government

A **government** is a group of people who work together to run a city, state, or country. (p. 174) Some people in our **government** work at the state capitol.

governor

A **governor** is the leader of a state's government. (p. 175) Every state has a **governor.**

harbor

A **harbor** is an area of deep water that is safe from wind and waves. (p. 29) Large ships can bring goods into a **harbor.**

hemisphere

A **hemisphere** is half of Earth. (p. 22) The Northern **Hemisphere** is north of the equator.

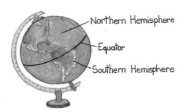

hill

A **hill** is land that rises above the land around it. (p. 28) **Hills** are smaller than mountains.

history

The study of things that happened in the past is called **history**. (p. 63) The **history** of our country is interesting.

human resource

A **human resource** is a worker. (p. 43) Office workers are **human resources.**

immigrant

An **immigrant** is a person who comes from another place to live in a country. (p. 72) My great-grandmother was an Irish **immigrant.**

Internet

The **Internet** is a large system of connected computers. (p. 118) You can use the **Internet** to do research.

island

An **island** is a landform with water all around it. (p. 26) Deep blue water surrounds the **island.**

judge

A **judge** is someone who studies laws and decides the best way to follow them. (p. 161) A **judge** may help decide if someone has broken a law.

lake

A body of water with land all around it is called a **lake.** (p. 26) Most **lakes** have fresh water.

landform

A **landform** is one of the shapes of land found on Earth. (p. 24) A mountain is a **landform.**

landmark

A **landmark** is a feature that makes a location special. (p. 168) The Statue of Liberty is a **landmark** of New York City.

law

A rule that everyone in a community, state, or country must follow is called a **law.** (p. 159) A driver who doesn't stop at a stop sign is breaking a **law.**

location

A **location** tells where a place is. (p. 8) The **location** of my house is next to the park.

map

A **map** is a flat drawing that shows where places are. (p. 8) Can you find the lake on this **map**?

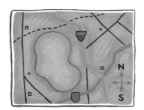

mayor

A **mayor** is the leader of a city or town government. (p. 184) The **mayor** makes important decisions for our community.

monument

A **monument** is a building or statue that honors a hero or an event. (p. 168) The Washington Monument honors the first President of the United States.

natural resource

Something in nature that people can use is a **natural resource.** (p. 42) Trees are an important **natural resource**.

ocean

An **ocean** is a very large body of salt water. (p. 14) There are five **oceans** on Earth.

opinion

An **opinion** is a belief based on what you think or feel, rather than on facts. (p. 126) In my **opinion**, soccer is better than baseball.

performer

A **performer** is a person whose job is to dance, act, or make music. (p. 93) Many **performers** work in New York City.

population

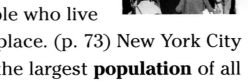

Population is the number of people who live in a place. (p. 73) New York City has the largest **population** of all the cities in the United States.

public service

A **public service** is a service that a government provides for all citizens. (p. 192) Police officers provide a **public service.**

rule

A **rule** is a statement or an idea that tells people what they should or should not do. (p. 158) One school **rule** says that you must respect others.

rural area

A **rural area** is an area in the country, usually away from a city. (p. 122) **Rural areas** have more open space than cities and suburbs.

settler

One of the first people to make a home in a new place is a **settler.** (p. 68) Dutch **settlers** lived in what is now New York City long ago.

shelter

Something that protects or covers is called a **shelter.** (p. 115) Apartment buildings are a kind of **shelter.**

skyscraper

A **skyscraper** is a very tall building. (p. 81) The first **skyscraper** in New York City was 11 stories tall.

state

Part of a country is called a **state.** (p. 20) New York is one **state** of 50 in the United States.

suburb

A **suburb** is a community near a city. (p. 121) Many people who live in a **suburb** work in the city.

symbol

A **symbol** is a picture, place, or thing that stands for something else. (pp. 16, 166). An eagle is a **symbol** for freedom.

tax

A **tax** is money paid to a government and used to pay for public services. (p. 196) The **tax** we pay at the store helps pay for building roads.

Baseball	$7.00
Baseball glove	$35.00
SUBTOTAL	$42.00
New York City Tax 9%	$3.78
TOTAL	$45.78
Cash Paid	$50.00
Change	$4.22

technology

Technology is the use of science to make things work better. (p. 80) Wind turbines are a new **technology** that make electricity.

timeline

A **timeline** is an ordered group of words and dates that shows when events happened. (p. 78) A **timeline** must be divided into equal parts.

tourism

Tourism is the business of helping visitors. (p. 94) Hotel clerks and tour bus operators work in **tourism.**

transportation

The moving of people and things from place to place is called **transportation.** (p. 37) A car is one form of **transportation.**

tunnel

A **tunnel** is a path that runs through or under something. (p. 36) Subway trains run through **tunnels.**

urban area

Urban area is another name for a city. (p. 120) An **urban area** has many people and buildings.

valley

The low land between mountains or hills is called a **valley.** (p. 25) A **valley** often has a river running through it.

vote

To **vote** means to show or make a choice for a leader or law. (p. 176) You may **vote** for class president or team captain.

waterway

A **waterway** is a body of water that boats can use. (p. 34) New York City's **waterways** include rivers, bays, canals, and the ocean.

Index

Page numbers following an italicized *m* refer to maps.

Index

Index

Credits

Photography Credits

KEY: (t) top, (b) bottom, (l) left, (r) right, (c) center, (bg) background, (fg) foreground, (i) inset

xvi (b) ©Blend Images/Alamy; 1 (bg) ©MBI/Alamy; 2 (t) ©altrendo travel/Stockbyte/Getty Images; 2 (cl) ©Robert Quinlan/Alamy; 3 (tr) ©Atlantide Phototravel/Corbis; 4 (br) © EmmePi Travel/Alamy; 7 (cl) ©Richard Cooper/Alamy; 9 (tr) ©Stephen Mallon; 9 (tl) ©Stock Connection Blue/Alamy; 11 (t) ©Nicolas Rung - Aero/Alamy; 12 (b) ©David Pollack/K.J. Historical/Corbis; 13 (tr) ©Underwood & Underwood/Corbis; 13 (tl) ©Underwood & Underwood/Corbis; 14 (cr) ©PhotoDisc/Getty Images; 16 (br) ©PhotoDisc/Getty Images; 22 (cr) ©PhotoDisc/Getty Images; 24 (b) ©Andrew Penner; 25 (t) ©Richard Cooper/Alamy; 26 (br) ©U.S. Fish and Wildlife Service; 26 (cl) ©Rolf Richardson/Alamy; 27 (t) ©Tom O'Connell - Cloudview Images/Alamy; 28 (b) ©Alamy; 29 (tl) ©Bloomberg via Getty Images; 29 (tr) ©Patrick Batchelder/Alamy; 30 (tr) ©Getty Images/PhotoDisc; 30 (b) ©Mitsuaki Iwago; 31 (t) ©Sandra Baker/Alamy; 32 (r) ©Gamma-Keystone via Getty Images; 33 (tr) ©Brooklyn Museum/Corbis; 33 (tl) ©Brooklyn Museum/Corbis; 34 (b) ©Alamy; 36 (bg) ©Alamy; 37 (t) ©Marka/Alamy; 38 (t) ©Corbis; 38 (br) ©Image Ideas/Jupiterimages/Getty Images; 39 (t) ©Buena Vista Images; 40 (b) ©Prisma Bildagentur AG/Alamy; 43 (b) ©Alamy; 44 (t) ©Jess Alford/Getty Images; 46 (b) ©Frances Roberts/Alamy; 47 (tl) ©Stock Connection Blue/Alamy; 47 (br) ©Image Source/Getty Images; 54 (bg) ©Jupiterimages/Getty Images; 56 (tr) ©Patrick Batchelder/Alamy; 56 (bl) ©Getty Images; 58 (br) ©Martin Cameron/Alamy; 60 (r) ©FilmMagic/Getty Images; 61 (r) ©Getty Images; 61 (l) ©Frances Roberts/Alamy; 61 (l) ©Jeremy Woodhouse/PhotoDisc/Getty Images; 62 (b) ©Getty Images; 63 (b) ©Alamy; 65 (tr) ©C Squared Studios/PhotoDisc/Getty Images; 65 (tr) ©C Squared Studios/PhotoDisc/Getty Images; 66 (b) ©FilmMagic/Getty Images; 69 (tr) ©Samuel Cooper/The Bridgeman Art Library/Getty Images; 70 (b) ©Aurora Photos/Alamy; 72 (b) ©Getty Images; 73 (t) ©Lebrecht Music and Arts Photo Library/Alamy; 74 (b) ©Bettmann/Corbis; 75 (t) ©Jennifer Taylor/Corbis; 76 (r) ©Bettmann/Corbis; 76 (b) ©Cameron Davidson/Corbis; 77 (tr) ©George Eastman House/Getty Images; 78 (inset) ©FilmMagic/Getty Images; 79 (bc) ©Aurora Photos/Alamy; 79 (br) ©Jeremy Woodhouse/PhotoDisc/Getty Images; 80 (b) ©Geo. P. Hall & Son/Library of Congress Prints & Photographs Division; 82 (tr) ©ClassicStock/Alamy; 82 (tr) ©Andy Levin/Alamy; 83 (t) ©Eric Bechtold/Alamy; 84 (b) ©Eric Nguyen/Alamy; 85 (b) ©Comstock Images/Getty Images; 86 (t) ©Keith Bedford/Reuters/Corbis; 87 (b) ©dbimages/Alamy; 87 (t) ©dbimages/Alamy; 88 (bl) ©Frances Roberts/Alamy; 88 (tl) ©Richard Levine/Alamy; 89 (cr) ©Alamy; 90 (b) ©Alamy; 91 (t) ©Bettmann/Corbis; 92 (b) ©Corbis; 93 (r) ©Getty Images; 93 (b) ©Corbis; 94 (bl) ©dbimages/Alamy; 95 (bg) ©Bill Hickey; 96 (br) ©Russell Kord/Alamy; 96 (t) ©Alamy; 97 (inset) ©William Manning/Alamy; 98 (b) ©dbimages/Alamy; 98 (tr) ©Gu Xinrong/Xinhua/Landov; 98 (inset) ©Getty Images; 99 (r) ©Urbanmyth/Alamy; 99 (l) ©Digital Vision/Getty Images; 106 (bg) ©Don Mason/Blend Images/Corbis; 108 (cl) ©Mike Randolph/Alamy; 109 (br) ©Ellen Isaacs/Alamy; 109 (tl) ©Ellen McKnight/Alamy; 110 (cr) ©Alamy; 110 (br) ©Jupiterimages/BananaStock/Alamy; 112 (r) ©Photolibrary; 112 (l) ©Getty Images; 113 (l) ©Martin Bond/Alamy; 113 (r) ©Jon Arnold Images Ltd/Alamy; 114 (b) ©Visions of America, LLC/Alamy; 117 (tr) ©Getty Images; 117 (cr) ©Comstock/Getty Images; 118 (cr) ©Blend Images/Alamy; 120 (b) ©Photolibrary; 121 (t) ©Martin Bond/Alamy; 122 (bg) ©Jon Arnold Images Ltd/Alamy; 124 (r) ©Valery Rizzo/Alamy; 125 (t) ©Getty; 127 (cr) ©Image Source/Getty Images; 127 (cr) ©Corbis; 127 (c) ©Corbis; 128 (b) ©Mel Yates/PhotoDisc/Getty Images; 128 (bg) ©PhotoDisc/Getty Images; 129 (bg) ©Andre Jenny/Alamy; 130 (l) ©Andre Jenny/Alamy; 131 (br) ©Alamy; 133 (cl) ©Transtock Inc./Alamy; 133 (cr) ©Alamy; 135 (t) ©Joseph Scherschel/Getty Images; 136 (bg) ©David R. Frazier Photolibrary, Inc./Alamy; 138 (tr) ©David R. Frazier/Photolibrary, Inc/Alamy; 138 (bg) ©Organics image library/Alamy; 138 (bl) ©Alamy; 139 (t) ©Owaki - Kulla/Corbis; 139 (br) ©Artville/Getty Images; 141 (c) ©Alamy; 142 (cr) ©Corbis; 142 (tl) ©PhotoDisc/Getty Images; 142 (bl) ©PhotoDisc/Getty Images; 143 ©C Squared Studios/PhotoDisc/Getty Images; 150 (bg) ©Ira Block; 152 (b) ©Richard Cummins/Alamy; 152 (t) ©Ted Pink/Alamy; 154 (br) ©Alamy; 156 (tl) ©PhotoDisc/Getty Images; 156 (r) ©Corbis; 157 (l) ©Andrew Gombert/epa/Corbis; 157 (r) ©Richard Levine/Alamy; 158 (b) ©Radius Images/Alamy; 159 (b) ©Gordon M. Grant/Alamy; 160 (br) ©PhotoDisc/Getty Images; 160 (cl) ©PhotoDisc/Getty Images; 160 (inset) ©S. Solum/PhotoLink/PhotoDisc/Getty Images; 161 (b) ©Getty Images; 162 (b) ©Janine Wiedel/Photolibrary/Alamy; 166 (br) ©Eyewire/Getty Images; 167 (r) ©Getty Images; 168 (tr) ©Brand X Pictures/Getty Images; 168 (br) ©Getty Images; 169 (b) ©C. Borland/PhotoLink/Getty Images; 170 (b) ©Robert Harding Picture Library Ltd/Alamy; 171 (t) ©Corbis; 172 (tr) ©Bettmann/Corbis; 172 (br) ©Peter Newark American Pictures; 175 (b) ©Richard Cummins/Corbis; 176 (tr) ©Andre Kosters/AFP/Getty Images; 177 (tr) ©AFP/Getty Images; 177 (tl) ©Jim Lo Scalzo/epa/Corbis; 179 (c) ©Andrew Gombert/epa/Corbis; 180 (br) ©Bettmann/Corbis; 181 (c) ©Bachrach/Getty Images; 182 (tr) ©Jemal Countess/Getty Images; 182 (b) ©Ron Sachs/CNP/Corbis; 183 (t) ©Corbis; 185 (t) ©John Lamparski/Getty Images; 186 (bl) ©Frank Franklin II - Pool/epa/Corbis; 187 (t) ©Bryan Smith/ZUMA Press/Corbis; 187 (br) ©moodboard/Alamy; 187 (bg) ©Yvonne Duffe/Alamy; 187 (inset) ©Comstock/Getty Images/Getty Images; 188 (bl) ©Elena Elisseeva/Alamy; 188 (br) ©David Katzenstein/Citizen Stock/Corbis; 191 (bg) ©Alamy; 191 (t) ©Getty Images; 192 (b) ©Richard Levine/Alamy; 193 (t) ©Sam Kolich/Alamy; 194 (b) ©Michael Appleton/NY Daily News Archive v/Getty Images; 195 (cl) ©Mario Tama/Getty Images; 195 (tr) ©Frances Roberts/Alamy; 195 (br) ©Richard Levine/Alamy; 196 (b) ©Terese Loeb Kruezer/Alamy; R2 (t) ©Getty Images; R2 (b) ©Zandria Muench Beraldo/Corbis; R3 (t) ©Greg Cranna/Index Stock Imagery; R3 (b) ©Greg Probst/Corbis; R3 (c) ©Getty Images; R12 (tl) ©BananaStock/Alamy; R12 (br) ©Bloomberg via Getty Images; R12 (cr) ©Comstock/Getty Images; R13 (cl) ©Alamy; R13 (bl) ©Comstock Images/Getty Images; R13 right side top to bottom ©Sam Kolich/Alamy, ©Getty Images, ©Samuel Cooper/The Bridgeman Art Library/Getty Images; ©Bettmann/Corbis; R14 (cl) ©Eric Bechtold/Alamy; R14 (tl) ©Andre Jenny/Alamy; R14 (br) ©dbimages/Alamy; R15 (tr) ©Andrew Gombert/epa/Corbis; R15 (cl) ©Frances Roberts/Alamy; R16 (tl) ©altrendo travel/Stockbyte/Getty Images; R16 (bl) ©Pixtal/Age Fotostock; R16 (cr) ©David R. Frazier/Photolibrary, Inc/Alamy; R16 (tr) ©Hemera Technologies/Photos.com/Jupiterimages/Getty Images; R17 left side top to bottom ©PhotoDisc/Getty Images, ©Richard Cummins/Corbis; R17 (br) ©Corbis; R18 (cl) ©Blend Images/Alamy; R18 (bl) ©U.S. Fish and Wildlife Service; R18 (tr) ©moodboard/Alamy; R18 (cr) ©Vincent MacNamara/Alamy; R18 (br) ©Richard Cooper/Alamy; R19 (cl) ©PhotoDisc/Getty Images; R19 (tl) ©Brand X Pictures/Getty Images; R19 (cr) ©Getty Images; R20 (tl) ©Getty Images; R20 (cl) ©Photolibrary; R20 (cr) ©Ellen McKnight/Alamy; R20 (bl) ©Ira Block; R21 (tr) ©Eyewire/Getty Images; R21 (br) ©Peter Brogden/Alamy; R21 (tl) ©Eric Nguyen/Alamy; R21 (bl) ©Ellen Isaacs/Alamy; R22 (cr) ©Mike Randolph/Alamy; R22 (br) ©Richard Cooper/Alamy; R22 (bl) ©Transtock Inc./Alamy; R23 (c) ©Nicolas Rung - Aero/Alamy

All other photos are property of Houghton Mifflin Harcourt.